The Unknown

Reflections of a Millennial Pastor

By Rev. Seth Nelson

The Church Unknown: Reflections of a Millennial Pastor

Copyright © 2016

Rev. Seth Nelson

Published by Rev. Seth Nelson

Cover photo by Jennifer Nelson

Rev. Seth Nelson
410 5th Ave SW
Ronan, MT 59864
(406) 546-7323

Table of Contents

Dedication

For Otto, my little inspiration.

Introduction

I started writing this book because I felt compelled to explain why Millennials don't go to church anymore. If you read very far into it, I think you will find I have failed. My bad. As I started writing and thinking about the question I have been asked many times, "Why don't young people come to church anymore?", I soon came the conclusion that I simply do not know. I have some guesses, which you will find in the pages to follow, but I cannot speak with any certainty about why people in my generation don't attend church like generations before us did. I cannot tell you for sure why your kids or grandkids won't darken the church door on Sunday, bring their children to learn about the Bible, or learn the age old hymns like they used.

But, this is not so bad, and probably is to be expected. I mean, can you offer an explanation for why people your age do certain things and don't do other things? Can you offer an explanation for every one of your peers' actions, thoughts and beliefs? My guess is probably not, and if you think you can do this impossible task you just might be delusional.

Yet, at the same time, you probably have an idea of why other people your age might have a tendency to think, vote, act or believe certain things. People in any given age group have shared experiences and perspectives that influence them in similar ways. I was sixteen on September 11, 2001, an experience, combined with the years to come, that have had a big impact on how I view geopolitics, terrorism, war, Islam, and many other institutions in the world. Peers my age may have similar or differing ideas and beliefs on these same topics, but they are all influenced by the same experiences. Generation X was obviously influenced by growing up in the 70's and 80's and the music scene of the 90's reflected that. I am sure not everyone was into grunge music, but I am willing to bet that Gen X'ers understand its influences and popularity better than other generations. Not everyone had the same beliefs or responded in the same way when the Vietnam conflict was raging, but Baby Boomers understand how much it affected their generation. Though you could not say with complete certainty why one person showed up to serve when drafted while another held out in protest, the worldview of most (if not all) Baby Boomers is unavoidably influenced by various experiences they had around the war.

In the same way, I hope to offer a Millennial perspective of influences and experiences that Millennials share have resulted in trends, and how some of these trends affect the church. Though I cannot explain why some Millennials do one thing and others do another thing, I can speak to some of the ways that we perceive the world and, more importantly for this book, ways that we perceive the church.

Questions have come up more and more in the past few years about why young people are leaving and staying away from the church. While much as been contributed to this discussion already, I believe there are more things to be said. I mean to add to this discussion in two main ways. First off, there is plenty of room in this discussion about why young adults today don't attend church as much as previous generations. Much has been written about different things that people are looking for from the church in the future than it has offered in the past, yet I believe that there is more to be said about why Millennials in particular are staying away from church.

I am not implying that there is nobody who understands youth and young adults anymore or that everybody who thinks they do has it wrong. There has been a lot of good research and writing into shifting dynamics in the Christian faith. I particularly appreciate the works of David Kinnaman of the Barna group entitled *unChristian*,[1] and *Soul Searching* by Christian Smith.[2] These works provide excellent, well-researched data which helps one to understand trends of those who are leaving the church behind today, even if those leaving still claim spiritual commitments. (Spoiler alert, many who don't attend church anymore still identify as Christian).

Many people have written about the Millennial exodus away from the church, but there is more that can be said. People realize that the church has been a bastion of moralism for a long time, but may not realize that in a very short period of time, the church's focus on how people should live has turned perceptions against it as a place which harbors judgment instead of a place that fosters the good. Where once the church was seen as the central place in American society where children can learn to be good and honest individuals with exemplary character, the moral teachings of the church are now viewed as weapons of judgment. Many young adults and youth have left or are leaving the church because they view the church as a place of hate mongering rather than a place where one learns to follow Jesus' teaching that the greatest commandments are, "You shall love the Lord your God with all your heart, and with all your soul, and with all your strength, and with all your mind; and your neighbor as yourself" (Luke 10:28).

The research that has been done is important, accurate and should be taken to heart because it highlights that the idea of going to church is hard for

[1] Kinnaman, David, and Gabe Lyons. *unChristian: What a New Generation Really Thinks About Christianity...and Why It Matters*. Reprint edition. Grand Rapids, Mich.: Baker Books, 2012.

[2] Smith, Christian. *Soul Searching: The Religious and Spiritual Lives of American Teenagers*. Oxford University Press, 2005.

many Millennials to get behind these days. Many peers of my generation look at me rather quizzically when I tell them that I am a Christian pastor in the Lutheran church. It is fairly easy for me to mingle with a variety of people and be 'one of the guys' at football games or hanging out at the bar. However, when it comes to the topic of what I do for a living, my peers are most often at a loss for how to speak with me about what I do. They simply do not know how to talk about the church, which I obviously hold dear. It is as if they do not know to speak about it without insulting my career and my faith. And this in a country that is still composed of mostly Christians![3] When I told friends my age that I was going to seminary, they responded, "Why are you going to do that?", and "Most of the pastors I know are pretty weird and seem like they cannot do anything else. You have options. Why are you going to be a pastor?" Other peer responses include, "Don't you know the church is dying?" and, a little more uplifting, "If I ever went to church, I would go to your church". The last is my favorite, but reveals the very reality we are discussing here: "If I ever went to church..." This comment captures the sentiment of many people my age – they are simply not interested in the church and even less interested in being a part of the church in the future. Despite how people my age might appreciate me as a pastor, they will never be a part of my congregation or any congregation, at least not at this time in their lives.

Conversely, I receive very different feedback from Baby Boomers and members of other generations. Having known that I was called to be a pastor since I was sixteen years old, I have long been comfortable with

[3] Street, 1615 L., NW, Suite 800 Washington, and DC 20036 202 419 4300 | Main 202 419 4349 | Fax 202 419 4372 | Media Inquiries. "U.S. Public Becoming Less Religious." *Pew Research Center's Religion & Public Life Project*, November 3, 2015. http://www.pewforum.org/2015/11/03/u-s-public-becoming-less-religious/.

discussing my call with people I meet. All across this country I have been greeted with smiles, pats on the back, looks of hope and emotional responses of people being sincerely grateful to God for my call to faith and leadership in the church. Almost completely contrary to responses that I hear from peers, those older than me place great hope in my call to be a pastor and are excited to see me as a leader in the church. It is as if my call to ministry gives them hope that the church will not die, at least not completely, because they have met a young man who will work to keep it alive for a bit longer.

This kind of response is not limited to the United States. I was visiting a friend in Germany where I attended her Protestant church. At the beginning of the service, she introduced me in German to the congregation, including in her introduction that I planned to be a pastor one day. Immediately, I was greeted with the exact same smiles and looks of hope that I have received in the United States. I could not understand a word that was said, but from the looks on their faces, those of the older generation rejoiced that there would be someone to carry on the work of the church. Likewise, Methodists in a congregation in Soweto, a township of Johannesburg, South Africa, looked upon me with adoration in languages I did not speak when they learned that I was going to be a pastor. The same was true in Namibia.

Perhaps, unfortunately, the generational disdain for the church seems to be international, as well. In Iceland, I met people my age in Reykjavík who could not fathom why I would be a pastor. They seemed to see the church as something to be aged out of, and the presence of a young person rising to keep the legacy of the church going was something that seemed almost disdainful to them. When I was in Sweden, friends shared that they desired to go to church sometime, but only in the way that they hoped they could visit museums in the country. For them, the church is not a living body of faith but a distant heritage that should, at best, be studied and, at worst, be left to die alone.

In my experience, there is room for not only more understanding of how things have changed from what they were, but *new* understandings of *new* realities that the church and Christianity are living into. I do not offer this work as a unique voice that stands alone. It is my intention to add to the work that has been done and to participate in continuing the conversation about the future of Christianity in the western world and the future of its church. To this end, I agree with those who say that we need to think about changes in our church and our world as movements which usher in new realities, not as threats to a church and world that need to be protected from the future. Our discussion should not be about how do we save what was, but rather how do we faithfully follow God into the future that we are being given.

The second reason I feel called to add to the conversation is that I believe that there is plenty of room for more *voices* in the discussion of why younger people have left and are leaving the church, particularly younger voices which actually care about the church. As with any conversation or discussion, the more voices included and the more diverse the perspectives the better. In these conversations so far, I feel mostly spoken to in negative ways. Negatively, older generations speak with contempt towards Millennials and how we are apparently failing society in many ways, especially the church. Older generations seem to have grown up with the expectation that as generations age, new ones should rise to take their place as leaders in communities, carrying out similar practices to how previous generations led things. This expectation has been quite obviously dashed in many Christian congregations, with a common cause being the lack of younger people carrying on traditions and practices that used to be standard. People older than me have often spoken contemptuously about the failure of younger generations to meet their expectations. This is understandable, but I do not think it helps to address the problem. I have spent a lot of time speaking with church groups about their desire to attract younger membership. "Great!" I usually say, then I ask the question, "How should we go about doing this?" Almost without fail, as we dig a little deeper, the conversation turns to something along the lines of, "Well, if parents wouldn't be so lazy and start bringing their kids to Sunday school again, then we could get things going!" The younger generations who are absent from many age diverse, church communities continue to stay away for several reasons, both complex and nuanced. Yet, one thing that does not help welcome outsiders or lapsed Christians back to church is when people in the church speak judgements against them. Nobody wants to join a community just to be hated by it!

On the other hand, I have also observed in my conversations with older generations that many people have a genuine, strong, and simple curiosity as to why young adults, Millennials in particular, do not attend church. They simply do not understand what has changed. I am often asked, "Why are people in your generation staying away from church?" The most important word in this question, and the most often repeated, is "Why?" There it is, the genuine curiosity. This is wonderful! Curiosity leads to understanding and understanding leads to strengthened relationships. The question "Why?", when intended with sincere curiosity, is one that leads to greater connection between different people, groups and, especially, different generations. Furthermore, I think it is a timeless curiosity. Generations of children, parents, grandparents, and great-grandparents have long struggled and wrestled over the centuries to understand one another. It is my hope that, in our time, we can dwell in a place of understanding how and why we are different from one another, instead of condemning one another for our differences. Perhaps this book will help as the church we have known enters into an unknown future.

Chapter One

The place from which I write

I was born in 1985, the same year as the original Nintendo console. This makes me a Millennial, a generation which is defined as including those born from 1981 to 2000. My brother was born in 1981 but said once that he does not consider himself a Millennial (probably because of all the bad press we get). I, on the other hand, embrace the title. When people talk about Millennials I have to admit that, more often than not, I think and act like a Millennial. On a basic level, I fit a lot of Millennial stereotypes. I dream big and try to be positive. I resist ideas of the suburbs and picket fences, while hoping that corporate types would listen to my good ideas just because they are good ideas, not caring about paying my dues first. I question a lot of older ideas, and spend a huge amount of my time distracted by Facebook and a myriad of other apps on my cell phone.

In other ways though, I do not fit the bill of a Millennial at all. I have no man bun, and am gainfully employed in a traditional position in a traditional community. While many of my peers have put off getting married, I was happily married by the time I was 23. I am not a member of the Rotary Club (I am not even sure if they have a chapter in my town), but I have been a lifelong church member, help out with youth clubs, am actively involved in the wider community and have voted in most every election possible. I am not as apathetic as my generation is stereotyped to be. While I think and act like a Millennial in many ways, in other ways I am much more than sociologists want to limit me to be when categorizing my generation.

If we are being honest about my life story, I am probably the least interesting person to write this book. I have never had to come up very far on the social and economic ladder. I have not suffered abuse, had to emerge from poverty, or overcome extreme obstacles to get by. I have never been imprisoned or been a slave to addiction. Sure, I have worked hard in order to accomplish the things I have achieved, yet I come from a lily white world with few hardships to be overcome. I have never been shot at or discriminated against, faced violence at home, been denied entry into any job or position that I wanted because of my skin color, gender, or background. In terms of interesting back stories, I have little to share.

I am a blond male with blue eyes, who is 31 years old. I am six feet four inches tall and am easy enough on the eyes (or so I am told). In terms of white privilege, I have a lot of it. I grew up in Iowa, went off to college, worked there for a couple of years after I graduated, then I headed back to Iowa to begin seminary. I recently graduated from there and am currently working in my first call as a pastor of a congregation in western Montana. If I were born at most any other time in American history, my story would be the most boring one you could imagine. Yet, we live in a time when it is a pretty odd thing for a 31 year-old, well-educated white male with a sociable personality to go into full-time ministry in a mainline church. There are a variety of other careers that pay much better and are easier to do than my current line of work. These days, people with my background are far more likely to be therapists, lawyers or non-profit workers than they are to be pastors. These days, my vocational journey is an odd one.

So, how did I end up on the road to being a full-time pastor in a shrinking, mainline church body which values traditions that many people have long considered irrelevant? For one thing, I was raised in the Lutheran church. From my very beginnings, I was raised to be a Christian who actively attends church. I was baptized in my first year of life, attended Sunday school, worshiped with my family, was obliged to attend confirmation classes in our congregation, and was active in many of the programs that our church had to offer. There was never a time that I have not been a part of the church.

Again, this is one of the reasons the back story of my call process seems painfully obvious and dull. (Where is the literary intrigue in saying, "Everything worked out well for me so listen to my story"?) However, this piece of my history has new relevance in our day and age as I am one of the increasingly few members of my peer group left in the church, and especially one of the few to join the ranks of the clergy. There are many who grew up in the same way as I did, but almost just as many who have left the church. Lots of people my age were raised in very similar circumstances, came to church just as often, but now have lost the faith (if they have really had it in the first place).

Why has this happened? Why are so many people my age backing away from the church? Why is the Christian faith and the Christian church so much more unappealing than it used to be? Why, in spite of this, do some Millennials buck the trend and continue to be active in the church anyway?

I am not sure all of the reasons why I went one way and many of my peers who grew up attending church went other ways, but we have. Not only am I still a member of the church, I am now a pastor in the Lutheran church – the first one that I know of in my family which has been Lutheran ever since the king of Denmark became a protestant in 1536.[4] As my

Millennial generation seems to have drifted farther away from the church, it would appear that God has pulled me into the center. Others my age who spent just as much time in the church growing up as I did, were in all the same Sunday School classes, choirs and youth groups, have now left the church completely. By doing so, they have made me less of a run of the mill church leader and turned me into one who has taken the path less traveled.

One thing that I am sure of when contemplating why I went one way and many of my peers have gone another way, is that I believe the Gospel of Jesus Christ has power over my life. I cannot deny that God loves us. I cannot live my life pretending that God does not care for every person in our world, especially those in the greatest need. Many have gone the way of disbelief or apathy, trusting in notions that God does not exist, but I have discovered that I cannot. Even if I would choose otherwise, I cannot help the fact that I simply believe that we were all made by a God who loves us. When I look at the brokenness of the world around me, I do not see the absence of God, but a hurting world that God is working to make whole.

This is not to say that my faith is unreflective or never been questioned. On the contrary, because of my belief in God, I would argue that my faith life has been subject to far more reflection, skepticism and even doubt than many of my peers. Feeling like a spiritual minority, I have pondered the realities of God more than most my age. When I bring up issues of religion with other Millennials, many of them report that they do not have much of an opinion because they have never really thought about topics of faith before. To those who do have strong opinions, most I have debated with tell me

[4] "Evangelical Lutheran Church of Denmark | Church, Denmark." *Encyclopedia Britannica*. Accessed May 2, 2016. http://www.britannica.com/topic/Evangelical-Lutheran-Church-of-Denmark.

that they have not really thought through their positions but just think the way they think and believe the way that they believe. This is not to say that these folks are in the wrong, I merely am pointing out that my faith life is founded on more than ignorance, contrary to what many of the "New Atheists" like Richard Dawkins or Lawrence Krauss might posit.[5]

I am not just a Christian because my parents and grandparents told me to be. Though my time growing up in the church serves as a foundation for my life as a Christian, my experience of being drawn deeper into the church goes far beyond this. From an early age, almost out of nowhere, I had curiosities about other cultures and ways of beings. I was far more interested in American Indians than in cowboys because their customs, cultures and lifestyles seemed so much different than that of my Euro-American brethren. As a young boy growing up, I readily and obnoxiously tried to be different and distinct, even though I lived in a small town that did not allow for a lot of variance from the norms. I was not flat out rebellious, but my curiosities led me to look for different ways of doing things. If something had been done before, I resisted doing it. Originality was the name of the game. I was full of desires to be unique and stand on my own by standing out from the crowd.

I suppose that part of the reason I developed strong faith as an adult is because Christianity now fits the role of dwelling in the land of the outcasts. The Christian faith has an odd, profound way of thriving on the edge. While Christianity has thrived at the center of American society until recently, the faith has often grown most abundantly when pushed to the edge. Christianity fits well in the hearts and minds of the unwanted, the uncool, the unfit, the poor, the weak, the sick, the imprisoned, and the suffering. Christ, who

[5] Holwerda, Gus. *The Unbelievers*. FilmRise, 2014.

calls the world to lift up the least in our midst, is easily received by those who are the least. A God who died to redeem the last first, is well received among the last.

Conversely, Christianity has often struggled to thrive at the center. Case in point, I write these words in America; the country with the highest GDP on earth in which the majority of people espouse a Christian faith. Yet, as a pastor I struggle to get people to actually attend our Christian congregation. Though Christianity still holds a tenuous place at the center in America, more congregations close than remain open or start every year.[6] Though some congregations and church bodies defy this trend in surprising ways, it is a trend nonetheless. On the whole, Christianity's place at the center of American society and culture is resulting in a declining church. This is not to say that thriving churches are only measured by maintaining or increasing membership numbers, but many congregations find it depressing when people stay away from our worship gatherings on Sundays. As a pastor, I do not aspire to have fewer members from Sunday to Sunday. Though there are benefits to the trend, the significant decline in church membership and participation is hardly a reason to say that our church is "thriving" at the moment.

Among younger generations, church attendance is now abnormal. The Barna Group's research shows that 59% of my generation who grew up in the church have now left us, while the number of unchurched among us has grown from 44% to 52%.[7] In many ways, this is gloomy data, especially for those of us who work in congregations. Those of us who love the church and have experienced God moving in our lives through our Christian communities desire for our congregations to

[6]Website: http://hirr.hartsem.edu/research/fastfacts/fast_facts.html, Accessed May 5, 2015.
[7] Website: https://www.barna.org/barna-update/millennials/635-5-reasons-millennials-stay-connected-to-church.html , accessed May 5, 2015.

do well in the future. These statistics seem threatening to the future well-being of the church, and they are personally terrifying to those of us who make the church our home.

However, many miss out on the benefit that these times afford us – going to church is now countercultural! While we are still a long way off from worshipping in the catacombs of Rome, we are no longer a norming institution in many people's lives. We get the opportunity to live in a time of discovery (or, more aptly put, re-discovery) in which the church gets to live out of the conviction of a smaller group of people who are committed to what they do in the face of larger movements away from the church.

As a Millennial, I guess I have seen myself as countercultural for a while now; countercultural amongst my Millennial generation of non-church goers and countercultural amongst my community of church goers who are largely non-Millennial. As a church going Millennial, I feel like I go against the grain in different directions at the same time. Often, I feel like my generation does not have a place for me, nor does the church. This is what my countercultural place between the church and my generation means to me; a sense of placelessness. It is from this perspective that I write.

Chapter Two

Not problems to be solved, but people to be heard

Millennials are frequently, readily and abundantly bashed these days for being lazy, disrespectful, rude, stupid, distracted, entitled, among other negative adjectives. A quick Google search for "characteristics of Millennials" revealed several articles, mostly straying to the negative. One of the first articles on the list in this search is entitled "Millennials vs. Boomers: Habits and Characteristics" in Parade magazine written by Scott Steinberg.[8] In the article, Steinberg starts by listing four characteristics of the Millennial generation; that we are (1) in no hurry (2) want more than money (3) free thinkers (4) falling behind. He lifts up that we grew up in an era of economic prosperity, but entered the work force in an era of extreme recession so we are kind of waiting things out. Yet, he gets more negative as he goes saying that we are not as ambitious as other generations and crave freedom in politics and religion to the point that we are falling behind our peers across the globe in job skills and performance. He then moves on to classify Baby Boomers with very positive characteristics saying they (1) say 'no' to tattoos (as though this is a real characteristic of a generation) (2) love working (3) are forever young (4) are tech savvy. In

[8] Steinberg, Scott. "Millennial Vs. Boomers: Habits and Characteristics." *Parade*, August 21, 2015. http://parade.com/417128/scott_steinberg/millennial-vs-boomers-habits-and-characteristics/.

his classification of Boomer characteristics, he praises the Boomer generation as one which has a clean image and works hard while maintaining a youthful spirit, even being surprisingly adept at getting up to speed on digital technology. If one could pick which generation to be a part of based solely on Steinberg's assessment, hands down, one would choose to be a Baby Boomer while being suspicious of Millennials.

As a Millennial, you might think that this article would get me a little worked up. I suppose it does, but it pales in comparison to so many others. A list of article headlines I searched includes "Narcissistic, Broke, and Seven Other Ways to Describe the Millennial Generation"[9], "Millennials are Pretty Terrible..."[10], and the widely read "Millennials: The Me Me Me Generation"[11]. Negative analyses of my generation abound, while praise seems harder to find. Perhaps the most positive article I found in my online searches is "Are Millennials as Bad as We Think?"[12], a title which still assumes that the reader already has a negative view of us, even though the article seems like it's trying to be positive. Terrible. Narcissistic. Lazy. Entitled. Materialistic. Overeducated but underperforming. These are all

[9] "Narcissistic, Broke, and 7 Other Ways to Describe the Millennial Generation [Updated]," April 18, 2013. http://theweek.com/articles/475383/narcissistic-broke-7-other-ways-describe-millennial-generation-updated.

[10] Edwards-Levy, Ariel. "Millennials Are Pretty Terrible, According To A Poll Of Millennials." *The Huffington Post*. Accessed February 3, 2016. http://www.huffingtonpost.com/entry/millennials-poll_us_55e87b8be4b0c818f61b1558.

[11] Stein, Joel. "Millennials: The Me Me Me Generation." *Time*, May 20, 2013. http://time.com/247/millennials-the-me-me-me-generation/.

[12] "Are Millennials as Bad as We Think?" *The Guardian*, January 24, 2014, sec. Media Network. http://www.theguardian.com/media-network/media-network-blog/2014/jan/24/millennials-generation-gap.

assessments that have been thrown out about me and mine. Not exactly language that makes us want to listen to other generations - descriptors which are more likely to put us on the defensive.

If we are being honest, most of these descriptions are true! It is a pain in the butt to get young adults motivated and committed to doing the work that needs to get done. I know first-hand in my work as a pastor that people I rely upon least are those my own age. Commitment is not our strong-suit. In fact, one thing that clearly defines our very diverse and ever evolving generational group is our non-committal nature. We do not want to be members of, well, anything. Even worse, we often look down on those who do commit to things. I am constantly feeling like I have to give a defense to my peers of why I join churches, got married relatively young, support institutions and vote. The anomaly in this situation is that I, as a member of a non-membership oriented generational group, will commit to things early and regularly. What's even more peculiar to people my age is that I commit to many groups at the same time. I sometimes feel like a barbarous Philistine for participating in society.

Yet, we are not the only generation to be looked down upon. I have been floored in this discussion when I study the era in which most Baby Boomers grew up in. Many of those leveling harsh accusations against Millennials were once themselves among the ranks of draft dodgers, pot pioneers, LBJ and Nixon protesters, and those who began the exodus away from small town America into the greener pastures of the suburbs. From what I understand, there was a time when the Greatest generation had nothing good to say about the Baby Boomer generation as a whole. I am sure families clung together well enough as the Greatest Generation condemned it progeny for not going off to war as willingly as it did, but things were by no means rosy between young and old when the Vietnam conflict was raging. The book entitled *The Unraveling of America,*[13] was not written about my generation, but about those who went to college and participated in the countercultural movement of the '60's. Many of those who were a part of the generation which *unraveled America* now attack me and my peers as a bane of society. If those who went off to college with a greater likelihood of getting involved in starting fires or blowing up administration buildings than at any time before or since could eventually get their act together and find gainful employment, then I am sure that there is at least a possibility that my generation who has suffered through far too many school shootings and terrorist attacks will eventually get their act together, as well.

All this is to say that, just as I am sure older readers do not appreciate being treated as a thing of the past, younger generations surely do not care to be treated as a waste of the future. Nobody likes to be put down, especially for others' perceptions that we have little to no control over. Nobody I know likes to be denied a chance to prove themselves. Whereas much of the Baby Boomer generation seems to have eventually cut their hair and entered into gainful employment somewhere along the way, the fact that many in the generation do not see this as a possibility for Millennials is frustrating and confusing. Give us a chance! Even more to the point, give us the same chances that you got. Don't prematurely judge us in the short term while giving yourselves the long-term benefit of the doubt.

Many of the generational judgments thrown around which critique entire age groups of people are usually only based on some members of the generation, some of the time. Categories of generations are usually based on the actions of a few, but do not represent people as well

---

[13] Matusow, Allen J. *The Unraveling of America: A History of Liberalism in the 1960s.* Athens, Ga: University of Georgia Press, 2009.

as might be assumed. For instance, I recently gave a short sermon series on generational changes in the church, and as part of it I did a little experiment. First, I said, "Raise your hands if you were alive during Woodstock." About three-quarters of those present that night raised their hands. Then I said, "Keep your hands raised if you were actually *at* Woodstock." Every single hand went down. Then I said, "Raise your hand if you were alive during the Vietnam conflict." As you might guess, almost all the hands that were up for the Woodstock question went back up, as well as a few more. Then I said, "Keep your hands raised if you dodged the draft or burnt down an administration building or anything like that." Every single hand went down. Then I said, "Raise your hand if you were alive during the days of disco." And, "Keep your hands raised if you actually ever enjoyed a disco song." Several hands stayed up. There were far more disco fans in western Montana than I ever would have guessed.

The point of the experiment was to show that major events and happenings which define eras and generations of people do not often define individual people very well. The experiment proved to me that it would be wrong of me to treat every male in the group who was alive during the Vietnam conflict as though they were a draft dodger because not one of them was. On the contrary, we have a couple members who were drafted and served honorably. Though protest and resistance against being drafted was a distinctive trend among many military aged men at the time, that trend did not represent the members of our community who willingly served when called upon. Just because I have read books about people dodging the draft in the '60's and '70's does not mean that I should go around treating every guy who was draft age at the time as though he had lived in Canada for a while. The same is true for my generation. Just because you read an article ragging on Millennials, or have a bad experience with

26

one of us, does not mean that we are all like that. Distinct trends distinguish groups but they do not define individuals. I am not lazy because I am a Millennial, just as not every Baby Boomer smoked pot in college or everyone who came of age in the '80's was addicted to cocaine.

People are as we are. We change in various ways over time, but rarely do we change because we are berated for not conforming to another's standards. Who wants to change their ways just because they are hassled about everything that is wrong with them? Worse yet, who is motivated to change because they are hassled for things that are wrong with *other* people?! Yet, this is the tactic other generations levy against Millennials. I am constantly facing criticism for the actions and apathy of my peers. Many in other generations find no problem in confronting me for how they think my generation is unreliable, for how they think young parents are not good enough these days, or for how they think my peers and I are not working hard enough these days.

This is frustrating for me because the context of these conversations undercuts the very criticisms being lifted up. Members of older generations have often cornered me at church and pastoral gatherings about the fact that people my age (in their opinion) don't go to church anymore. The context of these conversations is oblivious to the obvious; people asking the young pastor, who has committed his life, family and career to serving the church, why *nobody* his age goes to church. Nobody? What about me! I am here and not only attending church but *leading* it on a full-time basis. It makes it difficult to respond to these kinds of questions when obvious truths are so easily skipped over. How can people understand why Millennials have left the church if they cannot recognize the church commitment of the Millennial right in front of them?

People ask me these questions for a simple, sincere desire to understand trends that they do not comprehend. These inquiries, at least it seems to me, come from a place of genuine curiosity. The church is deeply important to Christians who have lived their lives in a faithful relationship with God, and many are baffled and even hurt that those following after them do not desire to keep the church going. It is a tough pill to swallow when one's children or grandchildren seem to have no use for the faith which has given one's life eternal meaning and peace.

Generations of church goers who want to see their churches live into the future pin their hopes and disappointments on Millennials. In a way, this is only natural since the generation which is most noticeably absent from churches anymore is the Millennial generation. The problem is not merely anecdotal, either. As I pointed out in the last chapter, surveys have shown that Millennials are the least likely generation to be Christian, and even less likely to go to church. To add to the problem of Millennial drift away from established congregations, many Millennial Christians who still do go to church attend age segregated communities that do not include people with many years under their belts, or do so only in small numbers. Older congregations are left without new blood to take over as members age, while new congregations of young folks keep rising up – sometimes literally across the street.

A big part of the problem though, is a failure of intergenerational communication. Old folks don't know how to talk to young folks, nor do young folks know how to talk to old folks. I have been in many awkward conversations in which people ask me, "What's up with people your age?" I have to patiently listen for what they are really saying, otherwise I would defensively respond, "What's up with people your age?!" I am a pastor, so I am contractually obligated to try to take the high road in these situations, but often times it is not easy to sit there and be bashed for having been born in the '80's. Instead of asking constructive questions like, "What do

Millennials want from the church?", "How might we be better at welcoming families with young children?" or "What do you think people your age would change about the church if they had the opportunity?", the more common question is, "What is wrong with you guys?" The problems confronting the future of the church are put solely upon Millennials, and frustrations that we are not creating solutions to the problems are deemed our fault, as well.

When it comes to bridging the gaps between those who still identify as Christian and go to church, and those who are in the "none" category (those without any religious affiliation), practices of critiquing Millennials are not helpful. Just as it is no fun to be berated into giving an account for other people in our age group, it is even worse for those who do not go to church to be forced to defend their non-religiosity. Those who are classified as *nones* are deemed so because they have no dog in the religious fight. For many of the *nones*, at least my peers that I have spoken with, most do not have much of an opinion on what happens inside churches at all. To question people about things that they do not really have an opinion about is a futile task, yet I have seen this played out several times in the few years I have been an adult – older generations cornering Millennials and asking them give an account about speculations and stereotypes about Millennial religious beliefs. I have heard similar critiques leveled against us over our supposedly changed perspectives of marriage, differing values in our careers, evolving approaches to education, or whatever other generational topic which may have been reported in the news lately. I am not sure that older generations mean to offend younger people in our conversations, but that is often the effect.

These bad practices of intergenerational communication are particularly a problem for the church. Christianity has always struggled to get people to come to church. Even in the height of Christendom, many towns built churches that only had seating capacity for up to half or even quarter of the town's population.[14] This meant that when the Christian church was at the center of cultural, societal and spiritual life in Europe, it was expected that only up to half of the population would actually attend church at any given time. The church has never been a place people travel to like they would travel to the Roman colosseum in the Ancient world, or NFL games in modern day America. The church has, for a long time now, been vulnerable to shifting priorities in culture and society, especially in western culture and society. The church has never expected that absolutely everyone would come to church (I mean, come on, there were always a few hold outs right?). Now, less than ever, can we expect people to commit to support the institution of the church.

So, whereas Millennials will still need to get jobs even though we are hired to work in environments where we are criticized for being lazy, we are unlikely to attend church when we are hassled for not attending more. Whereas Millennials are still likely to get married when we do find a person that we want to share our lives with, even more likely now than in past decades in fact,[15] we are reluctant to join faith communities that do not accept or support our relationships. Whereas my generation is still likely to have children even though we are criticized for our inability to be responsible parents, we are unlikely to bring our kids to church if we are not supported in our parental efforts by other people in church.

---

[14] Dr. Duane Priebe in a class at Wartburg Seminary, Fall 2010.

[15] Miller, Claire Cain. "The Divorce Surge Is Over, but the Myth Lives On." *The New York Times*, December 2, 2014.
http://www.nytimes.com/2014/12/02/upshot/the-divorce-surge-is-over-but-the-myth-lives-on.html.

I hope as you read this you are thinking of counter examples to what I am writing. If you are a part of a church community, I hope and pray that you do have Millennials in your congregation and that they are actively involved and feel supported as members of the community. Yet, this exception proves the rule. First, in my own case, some Millennial Christians continue to participate in Christian congregations *in spite of* the negative treatment that they receive from older members. These Millennial Christians are committed to their faith in Jesus Christ *and* committed to living their faith out in Christian community. These two fundamental elements of Christianity are not held up together like they once were; many Millennials still identify as Christian while not actually attending church anymore. Yet, some Christians in my generation still do. It is my assertion that we still do because we understand the importance of Christian community as an essential part of having Christian faith. Some Millennial Christians have a strong interest in liturgy and the unique aspects of mainline churches like the Roman Catholic church, the Lutheran church or the Episcopalian church. They appreciate how the liturgy provides a rhythm for their faith life and are willing to abide the critical comments that older members make about them because they still get to participate in liturgy. Others may love the music of an Evangelical church, others the fervor of the Pentecostal gathering, others the theology of trained clergy, and others may be drawn to some of the classes which a church offers. But, few of us appreciate being a part of communities that rag on us for being part of a generation that has a low church attendance record. Most of us who still attend church do so *in spite of* poor treatment by members of other generations, and have to fight to find a supportive place in the church.

Another challenging trend that reveals these frustrations is that many Millennial Christians still do attend church, but now attend age segregated communities. By *age segregated* communities I mean churches that are comprised of primarily young people and sometimes, unfortunately, only young people. These church communities thrive because they are places in which Millennial Christians can come to church and not be hassled for the fact that others their age do not come. There, they are able to be supported by other members without having to attend *in spite of* others' perceptions of their faith lives. I know that the phrase "age segregated" is a loaded one, bringing up images of George Wallace and other harbingers of white supremacism, but I use this term intentionally. It highlights the bad state of things when people of different age groups feel like they need to separate themselves out in order to feel supported. The fact that Millennial Christians only feel drawn to those our own age, in no small part because they feel driven from communities with older members, is dastardly and something that churches should work to change.

How do we welcome people of all ages to our churches? Listen to who people are and what they have to say. The world is made up of varied and unique individuals, and my generation of Millennials wants to see the diversity of interests, personalities, opinions, beliefs, doubts, and practices reflected in our institutions and in our churches. Unfortunately, this runs contrary to how many of our churches operate. In many congregations, the wide variety of individuals and gifts are expected to conform to certain shared standards and practices. Perhaps some of this is unavoidable, but I have seen that it does not have to be the case. I have seen many instances in which institutions like the church can be organically changed from within. When members of an institution take time to listen to one another, especially to hear divergent opinions and new ideas about the future, then the institution becomes concerned with more than one way of doing things and different ideas about the future. An institution which lifts up, recognizes, and heeds the difference that exists within itself is an institution which is not stagnant, nor one that forces conformity. Just as important, an institution which allows and encourages new ideas for the future is one that allows for the next generation of leaders to join its ranks as they are - something which Millennials are longing for.

As a church, we Christians need to listen to others with open hearts and minds so that they might tell us who they are and, in the process, discover who we are. Want to know what Millennials are looking for on the occasions when we darken the church doors? We want to be heard. We want to bring our hopes and our fears, our joys and our despairs, our concerns and our creativity to the altar of our Lord. We desire to bring all of these cares to the church so that these aspects of our lives might be lifted up before God and before God's people. We want to engage with our communities by thinking creatively about the future, not only being require to cherish the things of the past. We want to be respected and allowed to be who we are, even when the ways that we are defy the expectations of others. We want to come to church on our own terms, and be welcomed on our own terms, as well.

As a church, we allow for this kind of seeking when we listen to people in order to hear who they are, even if that means that they will still not come to faith or have anything to do with the church at the end of the conversation. As a church, we must listen to others to understand the variety and depth of persons that God has formed in this world. As a church, we must listen to others so that God might speak to us through them, whatever age they may be. As a church, we must listen to others in such a way that we enable people to discover who we are on their own terms in their own time. By doing so, we will be mutually affirming and supportive of people of all ages. A church community which affirms members of all ages will stop struggling to survive and start thriving together.

Perhaps the idea of giving Millennials more voice is the last thing you want to hear. Many people think we have far too many ideas already! Listening to creative and potentially new ideas can be unsettling, scary, and even seem unwise. None of us knows what the future holds, but we do know things that have been good in the past. Listening to what the next generation wants to do differently may seem like a risk that will only end badly. Better to pay attention to what has worked before than to change into the unknown.

Yet, if we take scripture as our guide, we can see that God speaks to us through other people all the time, usually through those whom we would not expect to be speaking for God. In the book of Acts, Peter and John addressed the crowds in Jerusalem from Solomon's porch and proclaimed to huge crowds the Good News about Jesus Christ. How many did he call to faith? As many as 5,000! (Acts 4:4) The priests and the Sadducees then detained Peter and John and brought them before the council in Jerusalem and were amazed at their words. Why? Because the apostles were uneducated and ordinary men, those one would not expect to say amazing things (Acts 4:13). God freed the Hebrew people and gave them holy laws through Moses, one who declared that he had a speech impediment. A refugee in a foreign land, Moses questioned the Lord in the burning bush about how he was to lead the people to freedom since he was "slow of speech and slow of tongue" (Exodus 4:10). The Lord used him anyway. The Lord even spoke to Balaam through the mouth of a donkey! (Numbers 22:28) If God can speak through the mouth of an ass, surely God can use the voices of Millennials to speak words of truth.

Chapter Three

A changing world means a changing church

My generation has grown up in the most diverse, globalized period of human history. Small differences in our American melting pot between, say, German and Irish immigrants a century ago, have given way to stark contrasts between Chinese, Korean, Ethiopian, Latino and Anglo-American friends by the time that I was growing up. The differences between country music and early rock n'roll of the fifties seem like they have little to say to those who grew up trying to figure out how European electronica, Tanzanian drumming and Latin Sambas inform our lives. The old religious differences between Roman Catholics and Protestants seem like a narrow conversation topic compared to dialogues between the plurality of agnostics, Muslims, Buddhists, New Agers, Christians and the myriad of different religious groupings that are now direct neighbors in our globalized society. Instantaneously, one can now see pictures of a friend's party in Norway, make a new social gaming friend in Japan, and read news from a local paper in Nigeria in a single moment.

The world is more connected, diverse, globalized, and smaller than ever. This fact is well-known, but it is difficult to understand how our increasingly diversified and globalized world affects one's individual experience of the world, particularly for those growing up in it. When the world around us changes, it is follows that our *experience* of the world changes, as well. For instance, when horses became readily available to the tribal nations of the American plains, their experience of hunting bison changed dramatically.[16] Instead of having to rely on a community to force the bison over cliffs as a group, an individual hunter could gain valor for himself by taking down one of these large animals alone on horseback. This is an easy enough fact of history to recognize, but what is often lost is how this dramatic change – going from being horseless to horseback – must have changed the warrior's experience within the tribe and between competing tribes. The young warriors who were part of the first generation that learned to hunt on horseback were surely better adept at the new methods than older warriors who had mastered the previous, horseless methods that their tribe had relied upon for centuries. This likely caused some resentment between the older and younger warriors as the new methods threatened the older warriors' hunting authority within the tribe. Since he could no longer hunt and battle using his pedestrian methods as well as younger warriors launching attacks from horseback, the new development not only made the older warrior's hunting methods obsolete but also his relevance as a hunter. The introduction of horses among tribal peoples of the Great Plains, while being an unprecedented and dramatic development, was experienced by older warriors as a painful diminishment of their status and value in the community.

The same was true when technology began to replace horse-drawn wagons and carriages with automobiles. Previously, most every community had a blacksmith who served in similar capacities as modern day auto mechanics. He would make sure that the

---

[16] Drury, Bob, and Tom Clavin. *The Heart of Everything That Is: The Untold Story of Red Cloud, An American Legend.* Reprint edition. New York: Simon & Schuster, 2014. Page 55, Kindle edition.

horses had shoes available, take care of several elements of the tack needed to ride them, provide metal hubs and joints for the carriages, and make other riding equipment at his local forge. With the onset of steel manufacturing and the rise of the automobile, blacksmiths became increasingly unnecessary for daily transport and work. As went the horses, so went the need for the blacksmiths who had to make way for auto mechanics to take care of the new combustion engines and the cars that they propelled.

Did these blacksmiths go quietly into the night, easily accepting that as time changes so does technology and the needs of technology? Maybe, but I bet there were at least a few of these hearty workers who had some regular complaints around the breakfast table about how all of their work was going to automobile manufacturers, auto mechanics, and steel workers. There was a period in history when horse and buggy travel existed alongside automobiles while every year there were more cars on the road but fewer horses. With each passing automobile, the blacksmith could see his place at the center of local commerce diminishing more and more until he had to throw in the towel and do something else because his business was no longer viable.

Does this mean that the blacksmith was wrong for choosing his trade? Did cars take over because there was an epidemic of bad horseshoes across the country one year? No, not at all. The role of blacksmith was essential in certain times and places, but is no longer because technology and lifestyles have changed. In place of the local blacksmith, the auto mechanic is now the crucial provider, helping many Americans to get from one place to the next without breaking down. Even so, the auto mechanic's job is radically changing with computerized technology, as we speak.

The point is this. When the world changes, we must adapt. We cannot live our lives pretending that things do not change because this is not helpful, healthy or productive. Whether it be the transition from hunting bison on foot to hunting on horseback or going from blacksmith dependent, horse-drawn transit to automobiles, the world changes significantly over time; a process which is drastically accelerated with the onset of certain technologies. The best response is to adapt to a changed world, not deny that it has changed.

More to the point, changes in the world around us mean that the church must also change. The church is distinct from other entities in the world, but it is not immune to the pressures that other institutions face. When the world forces business, organizations and non-profits to change how they do business, the church also has some decisions to make. We should not shrink back or pretend that things can be like they once were, but, instead, recognize that for the church to minister to a changed world it must allow itself to also be changed.

For many congregations, this is easier said than done. For one thing, the church is a place in which past, present and future meet together and have always met together. Believing that we are resurrected to new life through Jesus Christ who is at the center of the church, we believe that what goes on in the church is the same today as it was yesterday and will be tomorrow. When we worship the risen Lord, we join with the saints who have gone before us, those physically present with us, as well as those who will come after us. Those of us who are united in Christ are united in his life, death and resurrection throughout all of time.

The question follows that if the church is united in Christ through time, how is the church different from yesterday? When we talk about change, from what would we change and into what? From resurrected people into resurrected people?

While the foundation of the church has always been and will always be the same, Jesus Christ, the expression of the church changes over time, often drastically. There are many aspects of church life that look dramatically different today than they did a thousand years ago. From music, to clothing, to language – expressions of how we worship our risen Lord together are very different than they were a millennium ago and, I bet, are very different today than they will be a thousand years from now. These are natural, expected shifts in who we are as a church which should not be considered threats to who we are together if Christ is still at our center.

Perhaps a bigger challenge for thinking about how the church might change alongside the world is that many congregations are places which provide a spiritual constant in a chaotic, shifting world. Many congregations are places in which people have long been able to bury their grandparents, marry their children, gather as family at Christmas and Easter, and raise their family in the faith by gathering weekly on Sundays. Though the world outside the church has always been uncertain, many churches have provided a sense of constancy for their members through it all. For generations, people have been able to take for granted that the church would be there and more or less be the same while grain prices fluctuate, wars throw the world into disorder, and disease has claimed the lives of loved ones. In a way, the church has been able to provide solace from a chaotic world by trying to remain us unchanged as possible through time. The church has often been a calm amidst the storm by trying to keep the effects of storms from our doors.

But, if we are being honest, the church has always been changed by the changes in our world. No church has gone through any American war unscathed. No church has been able to whether the economic chaos of its members without feeling the uncertainty itself. I doubt any congregation feels exactly the same way about slavery, interstate commerce, the English language or a variety of other topics as we did 200 years ago. Change happens in the world and as people are changed by the world in which we live, the church is changed by our changed people. It is better to be intentional about the changes that inevitably come our way than to deny that we need to change at all.

A very valuable question follows that we should consider: if we choose to be intentional about the reality that our congregations must change, from what do we change into what? Questions of this sort have plagued congregations for the past several decades. As churches have faced declines, many have tried to become places that might be more appealing to members and guests in order to attract more people to join them. Changes of this sort have included dramatic changes in worship music and style, abandonment of liturgies and church traditions, creations of new liturgies and traditions, changes in marketing, as well as changes to many other aspects of what churches choose to do and who congregations choose to be. Some of these changes have worked well, and others have been a flash in the pan or flopped all together.

When we in the church think about choosing to change with the world, we also must think about how we change. As with anybody, we should not change for others. The church should never change to be something it is not, or to reach to some unknown crowd that we think we want to befriend. This approach is fake, superficial and will always be proved to be suspect, especially these days.

Instead, being intentional about changing with a changed world means allowing people in our changed world to be a part of our churches as they are. Congregations should not change who they are, how they worship, or what they do just because they think that somebody else outside of the church might like it. On the other hand, we should be receptive to how members of our communities have changed and how we might welcome others into that change. To change is a natural, acceptable part of our world, and the church should allow people to be who they are in a world that is constantly changing. Yet, that change should come organically through people in our congregations, not from trying to accommodate people we think might want to come to church one day.

Chapter Four

Things are not as they were, and this is a good thing

The world has changed and so we must change. This really should not be so surprising except on the rare occasion of someone thinking, "The world has changed, so the church must stay exactly the same!" I have not encountered anyone who would say this so conspicuously, but I have encountered countless Christian communities, many in my own church body, who more or less think and act this way. They think that things were good once, so the church should operate exactly as it did then and, when we face challenges in a changing world we should aspire to just get things back to the way they were.

The desire for the church to fight against change is understandable. In a world that is constantly changing, it is good to have some constants amidst the chaos. When everything around us changes, it is nice to have a place that we can rely on to be familiar. This sentiment is one that Christian communities should respect and pay attention to because many people look to the church to give them what them what the world cannot. One unique offering of the church is a sense of constancy amidst an ever changing world. However, I believe that if we operate solely from this perspective we will fail to minister to the world as it is and get stuck spending our time ministering to a world that was.

We should not only accept that the world has changed and adapt to it, we should also accept that it is a *good* thing that the world has changed. Just as it was good for the pedestrian bison hunter and those who hunted bison from horseback to master their own hunting methods in different ways at different times, it is good for the church to adapt today. Just as it was good for the blacksmith to be a good blacksmith in his own time and now a good auto mechanic to be good at fixing cars in our time, so it is good for the church to follow suit. Things that were good for the church in post-war America may not be the best things for us to be doing in the 21st century, and we should accept that it is good for things to be different now.

Let us look at the example of the people of God as they worshipped in the wilderness and then settled in the land of the ancient Canaanites. After being freed from Pharaoh's oppressive hold on them as slaves in Egypt, the people of God spent forty years wandering in the wilderness. During that time, they all lived in tents while they struggled to figure out what it was to be a freed people and what it meant for them to be God's chosen people. Part of this involved learning the patterns of worship that God had given them, which in the desert involved worshipping in the tabernacle that housed the Ark of the Covenant. The tabernacle was a tent in the center of the desert camp of the Hebrew people as they spent forty years living in the wilderness, learning to worship the God of their ancestor, Abraham. The tabernacle grounded them when they began living as the people of the covenant with God.

The Hebrew people lived in tents and God lived in a tent. The people were nomadic, moving from one place to another to find water and other necessities as they struggled to survive in the wilderness. The Lord, their God, was just as nomadic as they were. The Lord lived in a tent and moved from one place to another in the same way as they did. The Lord did not demand a heavy statue be created for the people to worship and haul through the sand (that would be rough!). Nor did the Lord remain far off somewhere in heaven while the people moved to and fro. God dwelt with them and moved with them until they entered the promised land.

When they arrived in the promised land, God remained in the tabernacle for many years, but as the people of God became established in the land they sought to build a temple for their Lord (2 Samuel 7:2). The Lord eventually granted their request, saying that King Solomon was the one to build the temple. When the people settled in the land, the Lord settled there with them. They built houses, defensive walls, farms, and markets. After they had begun getting settled, the kings requested to build God a temple in kind, and the Lord allowed it. When the people of God were established, the dwelling place of the Lord was established, as well.

Did the construction of the temple mean that it was wrong for the people to house God in the tabernacle all those years? Had the people been worshipping the Lord in sinful and misguided ways all those years? Or, worse yet, were the people sinning by building the Lord a temple?

The simple answer to these questions is no. The Lord commanded the people to build a tabernacle in the book of Exodus (35:4-19) and, later, commanded King Solomon to build the temple (1 Kings 1). When the people lived, traveled and dwelt in the desert, the Lord lived, traveled and dwelt with them there in like manner. When the people were settled, constructed buildings, fortifications, and palaces, the Lord instructed them how the temple was to be built in Jerusalem where the Lord was to dwell in the promised land just like they did.

In these examples from scripture, we can see that God ordered the Israelites to construct different dwelling places for God at different times because it was *good* for them to do so. At one time, it was *good* for God to dwell in a tent, living nomadically among the people. At another time, it was *good* for the people to build the temple in Jerusalem where God was pleased to dwell. As the Lord moves, so moves the world; and, sometimes, when we move in the world, so moves the Lord. This is not something to be lamented, but embraced.

The church in our time seems to be moving in the opposite direction of the ancient Israelites in the desert. The church is now moving from established houses of God like the temple of King Solomon back to more nomadic, unsettled places like the tabernacle. In our time, Solomon's Temple is analogous to church buildings with long histories of housing full-time pastors and church staff. The church as temple can (or could) afford to have established programs like Sunday School, Vacation Bible School and a quilting group. The church as temple finds what works and repeats these traditions year after year. There is nothing wrong with the church as temple, but this model of doing things is widely and rapidly being threatened. It is harder and harder for many long standing congregations to afford sufficient staff or even to afford a single pastor. Sunday School programs and vacation Bible school events which once thrived are now harder and harder to maintain.

On the other hand, the model of the church as tabernacle seems to be on the rise. A lot of Christians are no longer committed to one church body, one congregation, or, even, living in one place. Our lives have been inundated with a variety of options so that we no longer rely on one way of doing things. This trend has had negative effects on established congregations while giving rise to emerging ministries. Now, many people, at least people my age, are drawn to creative ministries which seek to worship God in new places and new ways. Like the Hebrews encountering the Lord in the tabernacle in different places as they moved about the desert, people my age seek to worship God in new places and different ways than before. Many Millennials are drawn to new ministry starts and creative models of doing church like house churches. Internet ministries are on the rise, so that people are just as likely to have a Christian encounter on social media as they are in person. Small groups, groups meeting in the local coffee shop, and a variety of ministries meeting outside of established congregational settings have taken center stage so that many people looking to be a part of the church no longer look to actual church buildings anymore. The church is all around us and, like God's days in the desert, the church is constantly moving from place to place.

I am not saying that one model, the temple or the tabernacle, is better than the other. Both the tabernacle and the temple were ordained by the will of God in their own time. We know this from scripture itself. When the people wandered in the desert it was God's will for them that the Lord's presence dwell in the tabernacle. It was also God's will for them when they settled in the promised land that they eventually build a temple to worship in an established way. Likewise, I believe that it was God's will that the church establish itself in the United States as people became more settled themselves, and now that people's lives and lifestyles are becoming more scattered, nomadic and disestablished once again, it is God's will that the church reach to proclaim the Gospel to a world on the move again. This does not mean we need to abandon our pastors (please don't!) or our congregations. We do not need to get rid of the pulpit in order to share the Gospel on Facebook. Yet, our established pastors and congregations need to reach out beyond themselves to engage a rapidly moving and changing world. We need to look beyond the members of our established communities and be willing to rethink the ways in which we proclaim the Gospel to the world around us.

Some people have difficulty with this. I grew up in a congregational community that often struggled to accept new ideas and creative ways of doing ministry. They are not alone. I am sure that some people complained about having to worship the God who freed them from slavery in the tabernacle while others complained that God was restricted when the ark of the covenant was permanently housed in Solomon's temple. God is not guided by our complaints, though, and we should embrace the reality that God moves in the life of the church differently at different times, however we may feel about it.

Chapter Five

Exodus from the church had to happen

Many people in America and other western countries easily get lured into the trap of thinking in linear terms about how things change over time. A common belief of the sort that I am referring to is a belief in progress. Whether it be moral progress, intellectual progress, technological progress, or developmental progress, many people look to the future and think that we will just get better at things over time. People get caught up thinking that since Americans thought one way about slavery at one time, but moved to accept the truth that freedom is a right owed to everyone, then we are continually progressing to be more moral people over time. This belief is further substantiated by other moral developments in society. As a society, the belief that since we went from not allowing women to vote to allowing them to run for office, went from actively legislating Jim Crow laws to passing the Civil Rights act, and moved away from McCarthyism into the post-Soviet era, then we simply go from worse to better. This linear view believes that we were in a more primitive state before and just keep getting better together over time.

Other people subscribe to a linear view of time but apply it the other way. In this way of looking at changes in the world over time, one believes that things were always better before and are just on the decline now. Whatever happened before was better, because whatever is going on these days is always worse. People with this mindset lament the loss of the good ole days, and have a starry eyed view of the past. They think that what once was, was always better and people just don't make or do things like they used to.

I have heard, over and over again, split second assessments of church history from both of these contrasting, linear perspectives of time. Some people say and think things like, "The church used to be really prejudiced, but we are getting better at being more accepting over time." One saying things like this believes in the moral progress of the church. Others in this camp say things like, "Our worship is innovative and upbeat, way better than all those other old churches," believing that genuine worship is something which is improved upon through time. They think that somehow worship was bad before, but gets better through innovation and creativity. Yet, others say things which indicate a linear view of time which views the present and future pessimistically. "The church used to be really central in people's lives, but now..." They sum up the history of the church in half a sentence or so, then follow their assessment with long diatribes about how the present status of the church has changed and what this means for the future. It is also common for people to say things like, "This used to be a Christian country but now look at us! All our problems come from people's lack of faith these days." People who say things like this think that the world and the church used to be all good at one time, but now things are going downhill. They believe that people were at one time faithful and the church played a key role in the life of the world, but has been in decline from that high point in one direction only – down.

History tells us, though, that overall participation in the church has long been dynamic with highs and lows. There were times when people, on the whole, were more active in the church and other times when people backed farther away from it. While many church goers who are alive today may remember growing up in the decades following the Second World War, when church attendance (both percentage and numbers) was quite high, there are also records of times when things were not so great. I recently found an article entitled "Why One Man Out of Nine Goes to Church". That's right, why only one man goes to church while the other eight do not. The year this article was published? 1929.[17] (It should be pointed out that this article was published before the stock market crashed that year.) That's right, at the end of the roaring twenties, only a whopping 12.5% of men surveyed reported going to church regularly.

The research was conducted by Rev. Charles Stafford Brown, a Congregationalist minister serving in Longmont, Colorado. Though his research methods may not be approved by current statistical standards, Rev. Brown nevertheless received 320 survey replies which were distributed to people in several towns and regions through ministerial contacts in his network. Out of the 320 men surveyed, only 35 of them reported going to church regularly. These results make one question whether the good ole days of the church are actually behind us. Rev. Brown's assessment of the numbers provided a bleak outlook for the future of the American church and the American family in the decades following the 1920's:

> Here, observes Mr. Brown, is first-hand evidence on the matter of "the crumbling American home, not to imply anything as to the crumbling American Church," and he wonders if a careful survey of their families by the eight men who do not go to church "would not reveal the fact that they have less solidarity, less respect for parental authority and

---

[17] "Why Only One in Nine Men Go to Church", Literary Digest, August 31, 1929.

example, than the families of the men who attend church and take their families with them. I am beginning to suspect," he says, "that the Church has a right to appeal to the eight on the ground that churchgoing is a positive force making for family unity and family loyalty and parental authority of the highest order."

Even if the numbers might be questioned by modern methods, the sentiment is very current. The idea that trends of Americans staying away from the church is a foreshadowing of doom and gloom for the church in America is nothing new. We have been here before and the church survived.

I do not mean to say that what happened in the church of the 1920's is the same thing as is happening today. For instance, I am assuming from the fact that only men were surveyed for this research implies that there was a disproportionate number of men who were visibly absent from the church compared to the number of women who still attended. The occasion for the research was most likely that Rev. Brown could see that there was a vacuum of male church attendance in the congregations he served. Fortunately, this has changed some, at least as I have observed, because there is not such an extreme gender disparity in churches these days.

But, Rev. Brown's assessment of the church of the 1920's is very relevant for how we view challenges in churches today. He looked the incredibly low number of men attending church and thought that it meant looming tragedy for the church as a whole. Little did he know that not many years later the church would be living into its heyday of the whole 20th century. Likewise, from Rev. Brown's assessment we gain some perspective of challenges the church faces in our own time and we can draw a couple of informed conclusions from it. First, if history is our guide, then we are reassured that problems the church faces in the present may not make for as bleak of a future as we expect. Secondly, and perhaps more importantly, we do not come from a golden age in which everyone miraculously went to church. Church attendance ebbs and flows, meaning that when church attendance is high, it can go nowhere but down over time, and when it is low it means that it has more potential to bounce back than one might expect.

If we accept that church membership and attendance is dynamic over time, then it is apparent that the numbers of those active in the church had to decline. After World War II, church participation in the U.S. spiked to a major high. *Gallup*, a major U.S. polling agency, has surveyed people since 1939, asking them if they attended church in the past week or not. The numbers are reported on the following graph:

Did you, yourself, happen to attend church, synagogue, or mosque in the last seven days, or not?

Yearly averages

■ % Yes

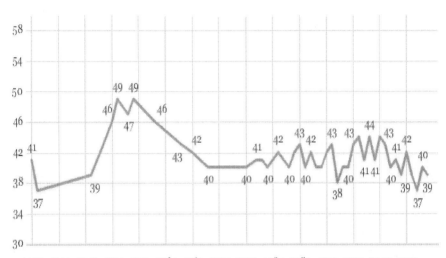

18

Looking at the numbers, one can see that, on the whole, church attendance in the United States has fluctuated between the 37% of those polled in 1940 to 49% of those polled in 1955, with church attendance averaging 39% between 2008 and 2013. The graph shows, though, that church attendance spiked in America in the 1950's and has settled down to around 40% of those polled. The research proves that church attendance ebbs and flows (at least among those polled by *Gallup),* and that church

---

[18] Inc, Gallup. "In U.S., Four in 10 Report Attending Church in Last Week." *Gallup.com.* Accessed May 11, 2016. http://www.gallup.com/poll/166613/four-report-attending-church-last-week.aspx.

attendance spiked to a 74 year high in the 1950's and 1960's.

Gallup's research confirms that church attendance is dynamic. While there was a peak time when the number of people going to church spiked, that number was never a constant high. Though the research does not go back to the '20's, it confirms that in the late 1930's and '40's, significantly fewer people attended church weekly than would start doing so in the following two decades. So, if we use church attendance in the 1950's and '60's as a benchmark to measure how the church in the United States is doing, then we are measuring ourselves by a uniquely high standard. People attended church in the 1950's and '60's at much higher rates than before or since, so it is not accurate to use statistics and trends from those decades as measurements for how the church always used to be. In reality, the number of people attending church these days may be closer to the average number of people going to church over time.

Perhaps even more importantly, these statistics show how different the church was when Baby Boomers were growing up. When Baby Boomers in our churches say, "People don't attend church like they used to," the research proves that they are 100% correct. When Baby Boomers were growing up, people attended church at much higher rates than today. Yet, it also shows that when they were growing up, older members of churches then could say, "A lot more people go to church these days than they used to!" The '50's and '60's was a highpoint in the life of the church that was unique, and, arguably, abnormal. So, if Baby Boomers use their memories of *how the church once was* or *what the church used to be like* as a standard to measure what the church is like today, then we will just be left feeling bad about the present state of the church. The church of Baby Boomers' youth set uniquely high standards that are hard to replicate. It is as if one were to go golfing for the first time ever, but judge herself as worthless and get depressed because she could not get as good of a score as Jack Nicklaus when he won the *U.S. Open.* I mean, sure, you probably would like to golf that well, but it is a pretty unfair standard to judge one's amateur scores by. In a similar way, to get depressed because people are not coming to church as much as the highest point in 74 years is not exactly a fair comparison.

The research shows us that church attendance more or less had to decline. Just as there are high times and low times in the economy, war times and peace times in global politics, and ups and downs in one's family life, there are ups and downs in the life of the church. If the church hit its stride in the '50's and '60's, then we should expect that church attendance would likely slow down a bit since then. It is unrealistic to expect half of Americans to attend church every Sunday for all time. As a pastor, I wish this was the norm, but time has proven otherwise.

On the other hand, this data also shows that low points in church attendance do not necessarily mean that worse days are to come. It is common for people to see declining numbers in church attendance and quickly conclude that if things were better before but worse now, it means that we are experiencing a trend of decline that will continue into the future. Notice, the research shows that *things were worse before they got better.* The graph shows that 41% of Americans attended church weekly in 1939 followed by a low point of 37% a year later. The years that followed included war time years, but a few years after that people started returning to church in droves. Fifteen years after the low point on the graph, 49% of those interviewed reported going to church weekly. The high point of church attendance in the 20th century followed on the heels if one of the lowest points of church attendance in almost a century. This does not mean that a low point will necessarily mean a high point will follow, as is evidenced by the up and down fluctuation in the polling of the last few decades, but it does mean that a low point does not mean that the church is dying. In fact, as was the case with the '50's, it could mean that it is being resurrected. Time will reveal what God is doing in our time and place.

On the whole it is important for us to recognize that church attendance in the '50's and '60's was an ideal for some, but not a sustainable reality for most. Though we might want the church to be as strong as ever all of the time, this is not the way of the world, nor is it the way of the church. The church is the living community of Christ on earth with its ups and downs just like the rest of us. When we recognize that church had its highest participation following World War II, then we should recognize that this high point meant that a low point would follow. Keeping this in mind, we can be reassured that though we are currently experiencing a low point in the church, this very well may pass.

Chapter Six

Jesus saves, not you!

"Jesus saves, not you." This simple but profound truth was put to my seminary class by our professor, Dr. Sam Giere. I cannot recall all the details of our discussion up to that point, but we had begun drifting into talk of our supposedly Christian responsibility for the faith of the world. Have you ever had a discussion like this? Discussions in which you think you need to figure out everyone else's faith so that non-Christians might get a shot at heaven even if they don't go to church or are from a non-Christian part of the world? Put another way, have you ever had discussions in which some say that they can't be Christian because they can't believe in a God who condemns people to Hell, others in the conversation say they are Christian but God loves everyone so everyone will be saved, while still others cling so tightly to words of exclusion in the Bible that they think belief in Hell is a cornerstone of the Christian faith? Behind all of these lines of thought is the notion that somehow what we believe about others' salvation has some bearing on whether God will save them or not.

Yet, as our professor aptly pointed out, Jesus is the only one who saves. Jesus said, "I am the way, the truth and the life. No one comes to the Father except through me" (John 14.6). These words are often used to push the point that salvation is found in belief in Christ alone and no other god or gods. Indeed, they do point to Christ as the sole being in whom our salvation is found. But, these words also mean that we are not responsible for the salvation of others. It is not our job to save others and any talk in that direction denies the primary role of Christ in the work of saving souls. I have heard several times from Christian friends, "I got so-and-so saved!" Or, "They are such a strong Christian. They have saved 50 people!" Complete heresy.

These days, there is a great generational push back over the belief that the church, its leaders and its members have an important stake in the salvation of others. The Pew Research center recently published a poll which got many Christians worked up because it reported that the percentage of Americans who self-identify as Christian had dropped from 78.4% of the population in 2007 to 70.6% in 2014.[19] This shows that there are significantly fewer people self-identifying as Christians than before, a nearly 8% drop in a mere seven years. The numbers confirmed the concerns of many Christians that the church is in a state of steep and rapid decline.

Yet, in spite of this, 70.6% of Americans still say they are Christians! These estimates mean that there are 172.8 million people who say they are Christian in the United States. That is a lot of people! How many of this vast number of Christians go to church on a weekly basis? As of 2013, only 37% of Americans.[20] Or, roughly half of those who say they are Christian are in church on a weekly basis, which means that only half of people in our country who identify as Christian are an active part of a Christian community each week. While another 33% report that they attend church monthly or yearly,[21]

---

[19] http://www.pewforum.org/2015/05/12/americas-changing-religious-landscape/ (Accessed December 2, 2015).
[20] http://www.pewresearch.org/fact-tank/2013/09/13/what-surveys-say-about-worship-attendance-and-why-some-stay-home/ (Accessed 12/2/2015).
[21] Ibid.

the numbers show that people do not seem to view participation in the body of Christ as all that important any more, even if they still identify as Christian. In other words, people believe that one can be a Christian without going to church and are exercising this belief by doing just that - not going to church, at least not regularly.

Much of the disparity between the large number of Americans who say that they are Christian and the considerably smaller number of Americans who attend church seems to break down along generational lines. The Pew Research Report on religious affiliation in the United States says that the Millennial generation has the highest percentage of religiously unaffiliated members. "As the Millennial generation enters adulthood, its members display much lower levels of religious affiliation, including less connection with Christian churches, than older generations. Fully 36% of young Millennials (those between the ages of 18 and 24) are religiously unaffiliated, as are 34 % of older Millennials (ages 25-33)."[22] The same statistics report the opposite trend of Baby Boomers and Generational X-ers, with seven-in-ten or more of these older generations identifying with particular branches of Christianity.[23] It would seem that Millennials are pushing back against the faith of older generations and doing so by staying away from the church.

In my experience as a Millennial pastor in a congregation composed predominantly of members who are older than I am, I have observed first-hand the difference in perspectives of faith and church attendance between generations. Many older members of our congregation have come to me concerned about their children and grand-children not attending church,

---

[22] http://www.pewforum.org/2015/05/12/americas-changing-religious-landscape/ (Accessed 12/2/2015).
[23] Ibid.

asking what they can do about it. (In fact, these conversations are a major motivation for me writing this book). There seems to be a divide between generations in which older persons were raised with the belief that salvation is offered in Christ alone and Christ is found in the church alone. Younger generations have come up questioning whether salvation is found in Christ alone and flat out rejecting the idea that Christ is found solely in the church.[24] Practically speaking, this leads parents and grand-parents to be greatly concerned with the fact that their children do not go to church, believing that their absence from church means that their children are not Christian. Will their children not be saved because they do not have faith in our saving God? This is a well-founded concern, especially when one considers church teachings over the centuries which declare at their most rigid that there is no salvation outside the church, and at its more lenient that to have faith one really must go to church.

The push back comes from younger generations which think that they should be free to believe what they want, and that Christianity is not limited to the church. In the minds of many of my peers, participation in Sunday worship or other elements of church life is not very consequential to whether one has faith or not. Many of my peers believe that one does not need to go to church to be a Christian. It is now common to accept that one can come to faith in Jesus Christ through reading the Bible, listening to preachers, going to faith conferences, listening to podcasts, participating in Bible studies at the local coffee shop, or whatever other way one can grow in the knowledge of the faith. For many my age, these alternate methods of encountering the Gospel are perfectly suitable while, on the other hand, it is an open question as to whether or not the Christian

---

[24] I am overgeneralizing here a bit, but I mean to highlight generational trends that I have observe.

should attend church. We have become a generation of Ted Talk pastors who are content to get our Gospel messages through our phones, but reluctant to receive them from the pulpit.

We Millennials, on the whole, seem to easily accept the truth that God can be encountered everywhere and anywhere, while at the same time being overly suspicious of the idea that God is only, or at least primarily, found in the church. Many of my peers do not trust that God is in the church, at all! On the other hand, where have other generations been taught that one must go encounter our God who saves us through Jesus Christ? In the church, and only in the church. Obviously, this has made for a problem of communication.

Let me set the record straight; salvation is found in Christ alone who is present in the church, but also in the world beyond the church. God's saving grace offered to us in Jesus Christ is wider than we can imagine and goes beyond what the church can imagine. Jesus may be encountered anywhere and is worshipped, in one form or another, everywhere. I have found God on the mountains of Montana, Wyoming, Namibia and South Africa. Gazing out from a high peak at the wonders of creation, God was revealed to me. God was present to me on the south side of Chicago through the cries of a mother and daughter holding each other to stay warm on a cold autumn night because they had no home to warm themselves in. God is present on the Indian reservations of the United States where many have been left destitute by the tides of history. God is present, moving in profound ways by showing divine love to people through simple acts of mercy and grace anywhere and everywhere in the world. God is present in Mongolia and Qatar, just as God is present in Italy and Brazil, or Norway and India.

I do not point out the fact that God is found everywhere to dissuade people from going to church.

After all, I am a pastor who leads service every Sunday. I get excited when more people join us for worship each week than the week before, and a little sad when people stay away. But, God does not trust the salvation of those absent from our congregations to our ability as church-goers to get them in the pew. Salvation is found in Christ alone; not Christ and the church, Christ and the new ministry program of the week, or Christ and our soup suppers! It is God alone who saves and God does not need the church to be hip or engaging or even very interesting at all in order to save anyone.

It is our job, as faithful Christians, claimed and forgiven by God, to proclaim the Good News that salvation is found in Jesus Christ alone, not to argue that people must go to church or else. Furthermore, for those with children, family members, and friends who will never set foot in a church (basically all of us), we should be reassured that God does not entrust the souls of those we love to our feeble efforts to get them through doors of our congregations. The salvation which God alone offers, God alone offers. Nobody else. God does not need our help to save souls. Hopefully, many people will become Christian and be baptized because they heard good preaching or had a powerful revival experience, but the salvation of the world does not rest in the church's ability to perform well. The salvation of the world is in the hands of our gracious God, who saves people according to His will and love, whether the church deems them worthy of salvation or not.

Chapter Seven

The church is more than Sunday

Rachel Held Evans, in her wonderful book entitled *Searching for Sunday*, had this to say about how her Christian congregation was present for her growing up:

> But even as a kid you learn pretty quick that church doesn't start and stop with the hours posted on the church sign. No, church dragged on like the last hour of the school day as we waited in the hot car with Dad and Mom to finish socializing in the fellowship hall. Church lingered long into the gold-tinted Sunday afternoons when Amanda and I gamboled around the house, stripped down to our white slips like little brides. Church showed up at the front door with a chicken casserole when the whole family was down with the flu and called after midnight to ask for prayer and cry. It gossiped in the pickup line at school and babysat us on Friday nights. It teased me and tugged at my pigtails and taught me how to sing. Church threw Dad a big surprise party for his fortieth birthday and let me in on the secret ahead of time. Church came to me far more than I went to it and I'm glad. –Rachel Held Evans[25]

---

[25] Evans, Rachel Held. *Searching for Sunday: Loving, Leaving, and Finding the Church.* Nashville, Tennessee: Thomas Nelson, 2015. Kindle location 341.

Rachel Held Evans highlights the beautiful pervasiveness of church. Church is not just the hour or two many people spend in a building on Sundays, but flows over into the coffee hour, the choir practice, the golf game between a few members, the unexpected phone call giving condolences. The church is found when a friend trusts you enough to say, "You know, I am not sure if I believe what the Bible says." It is also found when Christians pray with one another, glad for a friend in faith with whom they can bear their burdens to God. The church is definitely found in buildings and established congregations, but by no means does it stop there.

I would venture that many people in this day and age do not see the church for its pervasive beauty. Church is often viewed merely as a formal place; a place where you come to baptize your children, marry your spouse, or bury your dead relatives. The greatest connection that many have with the church as a living, thriving faith community is their attendance to the Christmas eve service with grandma after the family dinner, but this is usually just to go with the flow of tradition. This is a formal connection with the church as a formal place, not necessarily a spiritual connection with the church as a place which fosters faith and nourishes the soul. In its formal capacities, the church is a place which is extensively and exhaustively debated, loved and hated, but is also easily ignored. As a formal institution, the church can easily be held at bay. The churchgoing neighbor who comes to the door with a gift of baby clothes for new parents, the pastor who schedules his day to visit people in the hospital, or the member who silently helps another pay his bills, cannot. When church is just something to be attended on a Sunday it is easy to leave it there. When church is waiting at your doorstep to make your life just a little bit better, it is harder to leave it in the cold.

I have often heard it said, "I don't have to go to church to be a Christian." Perhaps you have heard things like this, too. In fact, whether it be in a conversation with a co-worker who does not have a faith home, discussions with adult children about where their hearts are at, or conversations with strangers about the nature of the church, this is an easy phrase to end unwanted faith conversations. It allows the speaker to claim a certain appreciation for the Christian faith, while rejecting any commitments to it. And you know what? This is a phrase that works because it is true! You do not have to go to church to be a Christian! In fact, regular Sunday attendance at church has not been a constant throughout the history of western Christianity. When the Roman Catholic authorities first determined requirements for parish membership in medieval Europe, they did not decide that members needed to attend every other week or once a month. Nor did they say that members were required to be at both Christmas and Easter services, a mere two worship services per year. No, the first official determination of what it means to be a member of a church in good standing was that members needed to come to church for communion and confession only *once* per year![26] This means that the church authorities of the time, and those following after them, believed that one could be a Christian without attending church 51 weeks out of the year. Clearly, there is a long history to the belief that one does not need to attend church to be a Christian, even within the church itself.

Yet, this is not the whole story, nor is it the best way to think about what is really being said when comments like this are made. As Rachel Held Evans points out, the church is wide and vast in how it is

[26] Irvin, Dale T., and Scott W. Sunquist. *History of the World Christian Movement: Earliest Christianity to 1453.* 8/16/01 edition. Maryknoll, N.Y: Orbis Books, 2001.

present in people's lives. Church attendance is only one mark of the Christian faith. I know many individuals who are hard pressed to get into the pews regularly, but are faithful tithers, nonetheless. I know others who have a hard time with the liturgies which are recited in church every week, but are the first to volunteer at the food bank or serve community meals. While many of these individuals live out the truth of the phrase, "You don't have to go to church to be a Christian", I have yet to hear these sorts of folks utter such a phrase. Those I have heard say it, on the other hand, are apathetic about *all* aspects of the Christian life, not just church attendance. It is true that one does not need to go to church in order to be a Christian, but this sentiment should not be used as an excuse for apathy.

Let me offer what I think is a better phrasing of this sentiment: "The Christian life involves *more* than going to church on Sunday". Church attendance provides a rhythm for our faith lives, regularly connecting us with our God and our neighbors in faith. If we agree with Jesus' teaching that where we spend our time and our money is where we place value (Matthew 6:21, Luke 12:43), then spending time in church every week is an important way to show the value we place on our faith lives. While it is good to recognize that one does not need to go to church to be a Christian, it is important to see that the Christian life necessarily includes what happens on Sunday mornings. The choice does not come down to a choice of participating in church on Sundays or not, but rather participating in church on Sunday and then choosing how we are going to go out to live the Christian life in unique and varied ways. This is what I mean when I say Christianity involves *more* than Sunday.

It is also important that we not limit the Christian life by failing to recognize the breadth of faith experiences that Christians have, and the myriad of ways in which people live out their faith. The Christian life is deep and wide. It includes making meals for those who have lost a family member. The Christian life includes helping out a friend who has just lost a job, gone through a divorce, or is experiencing some other sort of hardship. The Christian life includes a business owner who hires an ex-convict to give him a second chance. The Christian life includes quilting ladies spending hundreds of hours making quilts to ship to disaster areas in countries that they will never travel to, just because it is a good and loving thing to do in the name of Christ. The Christian life includes these and so many more ways in which we reach out in love on account of our faith. While many of these aspects of the Christian life are present on Sunday mornings, they really are best lived out Monday through Saturday.

Considering all of this, many question the importance of Sunday worship. Since we recognize that the Christian life extends beyond what happens on the Lord's day, why place importance on it at all? Why worship on Sunday? Why choose any day in which to worship instead of picking up your Bible any day of the week, or listening to the last preacher podcast whenever it is published? For one thing, Sunday worship is Biblical. In the book of Acts, when the early Christians first experienced the Holy Spirit poured out upon their worship gathering at Pentecost, they were gathered on a Sunday, the first day of the week. "When the day of Pentecost had come, they were all together in one place. And suddenly from heaven there came a sound like the rush of a violent wind, and it filled the entire house where they were sitting...All of them were filled with the Holy Spirit and began to speak in other languages, as the Spirit gave them ability" (Acts 2:1-4). Now, the day of Pentecost was calculated to be fifty days after Passover which means that the Holy Spirit was first poured out on the people on none other than a Sunday. At a post-resurrection Christian gathering on the day of Jesus' resurrection, the Spirit came down and filled the worshipping assembly with its presence and power. Even for the earliest church, God showed up amidst their worship gathering on a Sunday.

The details of this are disputed by some, and some groups like the Seventh Day Adventists reject Sunday worship all together, but the important fact remains that Jesus rose on a Sunday. Sunday, the day when Jesus was resurrected from the dead, the early Christians worshipped because they worshipped as a people of the resurrection. Still today, Christians who gather to worship our risen Lord are people of the resurrection. As people of the resurrection, it is worth fighting to keep our worship on Sundays, despite any obstacles (sporting events, fishing trips, a chance to sleep in, etc.) that may keep people from joining us on the Lord's day. Sunday is the best day for us to gather as a church to worship because it is the day of our salvation.

The better question to entertain is, why *only* Sunday? As Rachel Held Evans pointed out, experiences of the church are often more powerful and meaningful when the church comes to us than when we are expected to go to it. It is powerful and engaging when the people of God, inspired by their collective worship together head out into the rest of their weeks as faithful Christians who bring their worship to the rest of their lives. This happens when Christians bring the church to their workplaces by diligently doing their jobs and helping their co-workers in times of need. We Christians bring the church to others when we support friends who have lost a loved one and need the support of others in their time of grief. Christians bring the church to the school board, the city council, the voting box, or wherever else public life happens when we diligently work for the good in our communities and in our world.

What does Christ have to say to those who see the church as being found *only* on Sunday? In Matthew 25,

Jesus identifies with those who are in need, any day of the week.

> When the Son of Man comes in his glory, and all the angels with him then he will sit on the throne of his glory. All the nations will be gathered before him, and he will separate people one from another as a shepherd separates the sheep from the goats, and he will put the sheep at his right hand and the goats at the left. Then the king will say to those at his right hand, "Come, you that are blessed by my Father, inherit the kingdom prepared for you from the foundation of the world; for I was hungry and you gave me food, I was thirsty and you gave me something to drink, I was a stranger and you welcomed me, I was naked and you gave me clothing, I was sick and you took care of me, I was in prison and you visited me.' Then the righteous will answer him, "Lord, when was it that we saw you hungry and gave you food, or thirsty and gave you something to drink? And when was it that we saw you a stranger and welcomed you, or naked and gave you clothing? And when was it that we saw you sick or in prison and visited you?' And the king will answer them, 'Truly I tell you, just as you did it to one of the least of these who are members of my family, you did it to me.' (Matthew 25:31-40)

Jesus is found throughout the world wherever there is need, every day of the week. A church that gathers and worships on Sunday to then turn around and go to the poor, the hungry, the imprisoned, the naked and the thirsty, is a church that reflects the Messiah. Christ identifies with a world that groans in hunger, a world that longs to belong, a world that longs to be redeemed. God is not just the God of the righteous and the rich. Our God is a God who commands us to find our

Messiah in the slums and ghettos of our cities and the impoverished areas of the countryside.

When we members of the church seek Christ beyond ourselves, outside of our gatherings, in the brokenness of the world, then others cannot help but notice. Christ formed the church to be more than just a Sunday gathering. The church was formed to reach out to people and places which are passed over by the world. When the church lives out this mission by reaching out to Christ in the world beyond its own walls - Christ encountered in the hungry, poor, and homeless of our world - people recognize Christ in Christians.

I am not sure if most of the people in the world long to be welcomed by the church, but I do know that most people have deep and persistent longings to be welcomed by a community. What a powerful thing it is when Christians minister to this longing by reaching out in Christian love to find a place for people in the church. Addressing our natural desiring to reach out to God, St. Augustine wrote, "our heart is restless till it finds its rest in you",[27] and I believe the truth of this statement is revealed today as much as ever. In our increasingly churchless society, people's longing to belong is as high as it has ever been. What a powerful thing it would be if the church recognizes this longing and actively reaches out to bring the love of God to the longing ones, instead of waiting for them to find their way into an unknown church where they feel that they have no place.

---

[27] Augustine, St, Robin Lane Fox, and Philip Burton. *The Confessions*. New York: Everyman's Library, 2001. Page 5.

Chapter Eight

We still need the church

Rev. Nadia Bolz-Weber, a fellow Lutheran pastor, took a less than cookie-cutter path to the ministry. She wrote in her book, *Pastrix*, that though she was raised in the church, she spent her early twenties working as a comedian while trying to find salvation through the mental numbing of alcohol and the euphoria of drug use.[28] But, for all her trying, she could not leave Christianity completely behind. As much as she wanted to, she could not commit to full blown atheism. Her friends noticed. When they needed a pastor, they called her. A significant part of her call to ministry was the suicide of her friend, PJ, and her community's lack of a pastor. Her call to ministry was literally a phone call which went like this:

Sean, fellow comic and rower said, "Nadia. It's, um...PJ, honey."

"Shit," I said.

"I'm sorry," Sean said. We were all sorry. "Can you do his service?"

---

[28] Bolz-Weber, Nadia. *Pastrix: The Cranky, Beautiful Faith of a Sinner & Saint.* 1 edition. Jericho Books, 2013.

This is how I was called to ministry. My main qualification? I was the religious one.[29]

Her community of comics, misfits, drug addicts and worse, had lost one of their own. They faced grief like anyone else and needed to bury him as best they could. They needed a pastor, someone to lead them in their grieving process, and Nadia was the closest thing they had.

Why did they have a service at all? This is a crass question, but it is one worth thinking through. Why did people who otherwise had no use for the church in their everyday lives have any need to spend time and energy burying their friend? If they wholly and completely had no time for the church, couldn't they silently just let him be dead and that be the end of it?

I don't know all the ins and outs of why the now Reverend Bolz-Weber's community wanted to do a service, but it is clear that they needed somebody to lead them in their grief. They needed a sense of church, however casual it ended up being. (Incidentally, this experience was a very significant reason that she entered the ministry.) However unlikely, or seemingly far from expectations, people need a pastor and they need the church. Though this can be almost comically haphazard at times, just like a comedian leading a gathering of fellow comedians since she was the most religious of the bunch, people still have need for the church and its ministry.

While people are attending church less and less these days, it is my experience that most of us could still use a pastor from time to time. Whether it be for a wedding or a funeral, a divorce or the death of a child, people of all sorts have need of someone to help them through times of trouble and lead them in their joy. However people may feel about the church, we need

___

[29] Ibid. page 8.

others in our lives to say with authority that all is not lost when the world falls apart, and, on the other end, articulate how our joy transcends the moments in which it is experienced. We all have a need for someone to reassure us that God loves us even when it seems that the universe is stacked against us, and claim greater meaning in our joy when things line up in all the right ways. This is the role of a pastor.

The pastoral role is not always filled by a pastor or a priest. Sometimes the best pastors of our lives are not clergy at all but good friends who say the right thing at the right time, a mother who knows how to reassure a daughter when her heart is broken, or a random stranger who comes along to give a word of encouragement at just the right time. Other times, unfortunately, the clergy who are entrusted with people's deep concerns, griefs, regrets, etc., fail to be trustworthy of the office. Stories of this sort are all too abundant these days. Yet, we all need somebody to help us make sense of things, give us hope in times of despair, and to reassure us that God loves us and is in charge of this world that often seems to be a world gone mad. Though the role of pastor can be filled by anyone at any time, it is good to have people who are trained to fulfill the role.

While Millennial peers greeted my discernment to the ministry with confusion or even disdain, the story is different now that I am actually ordained. As I shared earlier, my Millennial peers did not understand why I planned to enter the ministry. For many, becoming a pastor seemed like something reserved for those without other options or just weird church geeks. While I am definitely in the latter category, there are several other things that I could have done instead of being a pastor. Yet, I have known for a long time now that I am called by God to be one, even though most of my peers do not understand my call to ministry.

Now that I have been ordained, these interactions have changed dramatically. While my peers previously greeted my discernment to the ministry with confusion and misunderstanding, once I became a pastor, they started to turn to me, unabashedly, for assistance. When peers find out that I am a member of the clergy, they open up with life stories, concerns for loved ones, and a whole variety of ministry needs. For instance, when I moved to Ronan, Montana, to serve in my first church, I did not really know anyone in town. With nothing else to do, I went to a few bars to hang out and meet people. Bars in Ronan, as I soon found out, are not places where people go to just have a drink or two while chatting with friends - they are places that people go to drink like they mean it. As you might expect, these local establishments are full of people who would not be caught dead in a church. Other than my presence in the bar talking to them, many there would have nothing to do with the church at all. Yet, when they found out that I was a pastor they would bear their souls to me like a person who had been attending my congregation for fifty years and had a few things to get off of their chest. Seeming to have no need for the church, they nevertheless opened up to the pastor like they knew exactly what they were doing. It is hard for me to go to the bar anymore to relax because I cannot get away from the ministry even there.

This phenomenon of people with no connection to the church feeling the need to open up to a pastor shows that while Millennials may resist being a part of the life of the church, they still have need for its ministry. Many of those who don't attend church still have enough faith to look to the pastor in times of need. Need for the church, its ministry and its ministers is present in even the most unlikely of places. Those whom one would expect would have absolutely no interest in the ministry, may be longing for it more than you would ever expect. It is my opinion that there are more churchless Christians than we realize.

As a church, and as pastors especially, we should embrace the fact that we are still needed. While some church goers and pastors may insist that those who do not come to church should make the effort to come to us on their own, it is good for those of us still in the church to engage the realities of our time. Instead of moaning about the fact that people don't come to us anymore, we should embrace the fact that we are still needed in the world and respond to this need by getting beyond our church walls. Though people still have need for the church, they are unlikely to seek it out if they are not a part of it already. Instead, we must go to them. The body of Christ needs to reach out with the arms of Christ to embrace the world around us. Many churches and pastors have started doing this with ministries like beer and theology or hymn sings in pubs. Others engage with society through city sports leagues, food outreach ministries, and a variety of non-traditional ministries that help churches and pastors connect with others on the outside. It is important, now as much as ever, that we be the church out in the world, the church who goes out and meets people where they are at. Put another way, it is important that we be missional churches which go to be the church for people where they are at instead of expecting people outside the church to come to us.

While this sort of outreach may seem like a no-brainer to some, I have heard objections to this way of thinking, especially from older generations. Many believe that people need to make an effort to come to church instead of expecting us to go to them. They think that if the church puts its energy into going out to the world we take away from the need for people in the world to come to the church. Church-going Christians worry that too much time and energy put in outside the church walls will world take away from the essential nature of the church as a gathering place. This kind of thinking comes from a time when churches and pastors had the luxury to think about how people should best make their way to church, but those of us in the church have no luxuries anymore. We should be grateful for any person who makes the effort to connect with us, no matter what way in which that happens. Since people are not coming to us like they used to, we need to get out and do the work of bringing the ministry to the people.

Will this take away from the church as a gathering place? Perhaps. No matter what we do, some will fear that ministry focused on reaching beyond the walls of the church takes away from the church as the central place for the faithful to gather. Perhaps they are right. The church that meets people in the world inevitably has different expectations for how people make their way to the faith. But I believe that churches which reach out in this way will actually make church gatherings more relevant. The world still needs ministers and the church's ministry, so let us serve a world in need.

Chapter Nine

The Ageless Good

A member of our congregation recently discovered a magazine advertisement which was published in the 1950's that she found quite interesting. The advertisement encouraged people to go to church, any church, because by doing so they would support ministries which help feed the hungry, provide for the poor, care for the sick, and all other sorts of good for people in our world. The advertisement was not for any specific congregation, ministry or church body. It was a general public service announcement; go to church, it is good for society. Wish we had ads like that today.

Though there are several things about our world that have changed since the 1950's, especially in the church, the divine calling for the church to be a force for good has not and never will. The church will always have as its bedrock the love of God who calls us to love our neighbor in kind. The church will always be a place where people who gather in God's name are expected to show God's generosity towards everyone they encounter. The call to minister to the world was not cooked up in the 20th century, nor is it a generational trend of our time. This calling originated from Jesus himself, and is the foundation of the Christian religion.

This call from Christ comes to us through the jarring, powerful words of Matthew 25, the parable of the good Samaritan which re-defines who a neighbor is, the story of the widow's offering in which the two pence of a poor woman is praised above the exploitative grandeur of the temple in Jerusalem, and many more places throughout the Bible. It should be clear to all of us people of the book that God desires for us to help those who cannot help themselves, because this is the love that God first shows us (Ephesians 2:5). We are called to be generous to the people that God has placed in our lives, not expecting to be paid back. True generosity rarely can be repaid and never expects to be.

A valuable example of this is found in the gospel of Luke in the story of the widow's offering:

> He looked up and saw rich people putting their gifts into the treasury; he also saw a poor widow put in two small copper coins. He said, "Truly I tell you, this poor widow has put in more than all of them; for all of them have contributed out of their abundance, but she out of her poverty has put in all she had to live on." When some were speaking about the temple, how it was adorned with beautiful stones and gifts dedicated to God, he said, "As for these things that you see, the days will come when not one stone will be left upon another; all will be thrown down.   -Luke 21:1-6

Powerful. A woman giving everything that she owned in support of the place where God was present on earth. Yet, while this passage is often interpreted to be a story in praise of the widow's generosity, we should focus on what comes next. In the following verses, Jesus talks about the temple being torn down. When we take this part of the chapter into consideration, it is clear that this story is actually an indictment of the temple proponents of the time. They believed that the temple was to be supported at all costs, even requiring the last two coins from a poor widow. The widow's offering was not a holy sacrifice, but was treated as pearls before swine when the Romans stormed through in 70 A.D.

and destroyed the structure which she had given her all to save.

Widows in the Bible exemplified the poorest of the poor and the most vulnerable of society. Not really having a place in the working world, women who lost their husbands had a rough go of it and relied on the help of others to survive. The widow in the story represents far more than just one woman with a meager two coins. She is the image of the most vulnerable of those in Jerusalem - widows, orphans, homeless, foreigners, slaves - coming to the temple to give their offerings, and, tragically, having everything required of them by the religious leadership. The Sadducees, temple priests, scribes, and temple guards saw that the temple should be sustained above all, even to the point of preying upon the last of what the poor widow had. For the religious leadership of Jesus' day, the temple of God was more important than the people of God.

The story of the widow's offering has new meaning in our time. The ministry expectations of those in the story were that the Judeans had to give *everything* that they owned in support of the temple. It was considered more important than anything else in their lives. More important than Jerusalemites being fed, orphans finding a place to live, and widows being able to be provided for, was that the temple be supported. The temple priesthood believed and taught that offerings to the temple upkeep were more important than supporting life itself.

Jesus reversed these false expectations by becoming the *living* temple who serves us. Jesus did not require anything from us when he became the temple for our sakes. He did not require food from the mouth of babes, the meager livelihood of those who could hardly provide for themselves, or the expulsion of immigrants from the homeland. Jesus required absolutely nothing of us. Instead, he became the temple of God for us out of his own generosity. Jesus became the temple in

79

whom God was pleased to dwell so that he may serve the world in all things, especially those who were held back and held down by the likes of the temple system in ancient Jerusalem.

Christian congregations in our day and age can easily and too often do resemble the temple system which Jesus rejected. The church repeats the sins of the temple system when all the cares and concerns of the church get wrapped up and focused on its own survival, without concern for those outside. The temple system expected the poor to provide for its upkeep without providing for the poor in return. The church stumbles into this sin when all we care about is membership, donations, tithes and other contributions to the church's upkeep, without turning around and caring for the poor in our midst. For instance, many mega churches in the United States have repeated the widow/temple dynamic by getting people to give and give and give in support of church growth while being slow to provide for the poor, sick, and homeless in return. Churches that pour all their tithes and offerings into the grandeur of the worship space, the wonder of the worship music, and competitive pay for pastors miss the mark and fall into the same sinful patterns of the temple system at Jesus' time.

The example of the temple system is very apt because the temple was not essentially bad, it just became systematically misguided. Supporting church growth and sustainability is good, but not if it fails to do good. More pointedly, supporting church growth is bad if it comes at the expense of the poor within our midst. I do not think that Jesus would have had a problem with the temple if widows could come there to get a free meal, clothing when their dresses were wearing thin, or education for their children. Instead, the temple took from them without giving back. Then it took even more, until they had nothing left.

Now, perhaps more than ever, Millennials have the freedom and sensibility to criticize the church for its failures – especially its failures to carry out the good that we are commissioned to do by Christ himself. Expectations that people attend church have fallen away, especially among Millennials, so people now have the freedom to step back and call the church out on its hypocrisy. At the same time that expectations of church attendance have lessened, expectations that the church practices what it preaches have increased. Sadly, the church often fails to live up to its own messaging. Congregations are stalwarts for people who proudly claim their place in God's flock on Sunday, then demean and judge others every other day of the week. Churches are great at raising money to build new structures, but can be very slow to give even small amounts to causes of the poor in their own communities. Churches draw sinners, but they also draw those who are dishonest and hypocritical about their own sinfulness. Many Millennials notice and want no part of congregations which breed hypocrisy.

This past summer I was backpacking with a few college friends in Idaho outside of Coeur d'Alene. Over our few days together, my friends and I shared updates on our relationships and marriages, job experiences, and thoughts on the world. In the beauty of the wilderness of northern Idaho, we got caught up on what was important to us while having a good time hanging out and hiking. On our last day together, one of my buddies and I got to talking about the church. This friend is also a Lutheran and, until recently, was active in a Lutheran congregation in the St. Louis area, even playing bass in his church's worship band every week. Not long before our backpacking trip, though, he decided that he was done with church. He is still a Christian who believes in God, but he is just done.

I asked him about this decision to quit the church and he had this to say. "I was playing with the worship band and the church spends all this money on the building and their music equipment. They have, like, top of the line amps and speakers. They have a really nice mixer board with twenty inputs, but they only use four of them. After a while I was just like, 'What are we doing? This is just a waste.' So now I'm just done with church." My friend saw that his congregation was more concerned with what was going on inside the church than the needs of the world outside its walls, and he was appalled. He decided that he could no longer be an active part of his congregation which cared more about itself than about others.

I hope you hear my friend's criticism of his congregation in a constructive way. He was concerned about the good that his congregation was called to do in the world, but was disappointed. This is wonderful! He had faithful expectations that God calls our communities of faith to be forces of good in the world. He did not walk away from his congregation because he no longer believed in Jesus or that the church has anything good to offer. On the contrary, his concern was that his congregation was not actively serving the world as God has called us to do. His concern was that his congregation was not being the body of Christ as God intends, so he checked out.

I imagine many, especially from other generations, might focus on the fact that my friend proved to be just as apathetic about church membership as is stereotypical of people in my generation. I hear over and over again, "What is wrong with your generation? You guys are lazy and can't be counted on for anything." I have heard many criticisms which condemn my generation for not falling in to line by joining the Elks Club, the Rotary Club, our local school boards, the PTA, church councils, etc. There seems to be a nationwide frustration that those who are now entering adulthood are more concerned with shows they like on Netflix than supporting the local theater troupe. People are frustrated that many of us are closer with the friends we make online who share our interests than our neighbors two doors down who we don't really like that much. Frustrations have been widely published about me and my peers saying that we are socially and professionally irresponsible and are more self-centered than those who came before us. With stereotypes like these in place, it is easy to focus on the things that Millennials do which reinforce these perceptions.

In the case of my friend who stopped participating in his Christian community, it can be easy to focus on the fact that he, in essence, quit church. He is part of a wider trend of Millennials not stepping up to fill our parents' shoes by taking up membership in established congregations, and it seems all too natural to place all of the blame for this on my generation who fails to meet expectations. After all, there would be no crisis about the future of the church in the United States if people kept coming on Sunday. It seems only natural to respond by blaming those who are part of this unwanted trend as the reason for the problem.

But, when Millennials criticize the church, it is my hope that our concerns are not greeted with resentment or blame, but with self-reflection and reform. Imagine if my friend's story was received with a different focus, one which listened to his concerns that the church does not live up to the calling which God places upon it? Imagine if his congregation was more concerned with making sure that the time and money which people give is used to help those in need in St. Louis and the surrounding area? Imagine if the church listened and responded to claims that we are a place which breeds and harbors hypocrisy by doing some soul searching to reflect on how we very well may be hypocrites, instead of focusing on the fact that Millennials hate us because they ain't us, as the saying goes? I think that intergenerational conversation about the life and the future of the church would be a lot different if it was focused on the better future that God desires for the world and everyone in it, instead of getting hung up on how Millennials are messing up the present.

On this oh so important issue, churches need to hear a few things. First, if Millennials in your community are wrong and your congregation is actively committed to doing good, show them. In our congregation, Faith Lutheran Church, in little Ronan, Montana, there are wonderful and vibrant outreach ministries that I am convinced young adults in our community have little or no idea about. Members of our congregation give generous amounts of time, energy and money, to local ministries which reach far beyond our church walls. We are active in supporting and staffing our local food bank, provide a free meal for community members on a monthly basis, support a local domestic abuse shelter, and wholeheartedly support our vibrant Boys and Girls club chapter here. Members of our congregation actively work to help others in many and varied ways throughout our community, but I am fairly certain that many, if not most, of the young adults in our town do not realize the good that we do.

In a way, this is not such a bad thing. I appreciate people who do not submit a press release every time they give a sandwich to a hungry person or a dollar to a homeless woman on the streets. There should be no hubris in service. Yet, unless your children still come to church with you and are active in these same ministries, it is unlikely that young adults realize the good that your church does. How could they? Many Millennials have not grown up attending church, and even fewer have been exposed to the wonderful good that a church can do beyond itself. Tell young adults about the work that the church does. Many of us do not understand the force for good that the church already is and have almost no clue about the ways that an active church can serve the world.

84

On the other hand, if Millennials in your community are right and your congregation does not feed the hungry, care for the sick, visit the imprisoned and provide for vulnerable people where you live, then you should re-read the Gospels and the words of the prophets in the Bible because God has called you to do these things. Jesus called us to do good in the world around us, loving our neighbor as ourselves and selflessly serving those who are in need. If we in the church do not do this then we are hypocrites. A church that does not serve the world, especially those in need, is just as hypocritical as our worst critics suspect. We are called by God to live beyond ourselves, serving more than just our own interests and desires.

The service work which the church does is an ageless good that reaches far beyond the present through all generations of Christians. From the very beginning, the church grew because it served a world in need. The early church in the Ancient Roman Empire grew with astounding tenacity, but it did not do so just because of good preaching or excellent worship music. What drew people in is how others saw early Christians serving the world. These first Christians spent a large amount of time and money caring for the poor in their midst, providing them with food and caring for any needs they had.[30] They started hospitals to care for the sick, especially those with plague. In times of epidemic, most of the rich and powerful would flee population centers for their country estates so that they would escape infection. Not so with the early Christians. They stayed and cared for those who were ill, literally risking their lives for the sake of others.[31] People outside the

[30] Stark, Rodney. *The Triumph of Christianity: How the Jesus Movement Became the World's Largest Religion.* Harper Collins, 2011, 133-135.

[31] Ibid, 138-141.

church noticed the good that those early Christians were doing in God's name and huge numbers of people throughout the empire converted to Christianity in order to follow Christ.

In Ancient Rome it was a common custom for Romans and others to leave unwanted children to die or be adopted by others. These adoptions were not arranged beforehand. Infants were literally left on hill sides to die or be taken by others who might want them. This practice was just as appalling to early Christians as I hope it is to modern readers, so they started orphanages to raise unwanted children. When Romans would leave their babies outside on the hillsides to be "exposed", Christians would go out, save them from the elements and give them a home.[32] By doing so, the church not only showed the love of God for infants, but also for women, since a majority of the babies left to die were girls. Our Christian church grew by raising unwanted children, and drew others to itself by doing more good than the status quo.

There are other examples that we can look to throughout the history of the church to see the straightforward truth that people are drawn to good people. This is especially the case for us Christians who serve the world because the God who first loved us calls us to show the same kind of love to all our neighbors. Jesus said, "No one after lighting a lamp puts it under the bushel basket, but on the lampstand and it gives light to all in the house. In the same way, let your light shine before others, so that they may see your good works and give glory to your Father in heaven" (Matt. 5:15-16). Jesus told us to call people to faith by doing good, saying that our faith is revealed through the good that we do. We Christians are called to serve our neighbors, any in need, because we have faith in God.

---

[32] Ibid, 149-151.

Let your light shine before others and people will love you for it. More importantly, people will love God for it.

I recently experienced the pervasive draw that service to those in need provides for those outside the church. Our congregation's confirmation group is composed primarily of students whose families do not attend church, so they do not have much knowledge of what the church is or does. At the group's Christmas party this year we had a grand time making cookies and doing many Christmas-themed things. In the middle of our celebration somebody I did not know came into the church asking for money to buy gas. This happens quite often where we live. Ronan is at the center of the Flathead Indian Reservation and like most reservations throughout our country several of our neighbors need assistance in one form or another. So, I took a moment to pause from our activities and, in front of these students at the Christmas party, made a phone call and arranged for her to get some gas from a local station at the church's expense. A simple gesture which is fairly commonplace for us. After I was done with this and returned to the group, our confirmation students were surprisingly impressed. "That's really cool!" one student said. Another said, "I didn't know you guys helped people out like that. That is awesome!". They were surprised by the ageless good that the church does. The good that the church does should not be taken for granted or hidden from the eyes of the world. When people see the good that the church does, I believe that many will be drawn to recognize its timeless value - for no other reason than it is a place in which people are inspired to serve the world because of their faith in God.

What's more? People, especially Millennials, need to be taught how to be a force for good. Learning how to allocate time and money at the local food pantry, volunteering to feed children on the weekends, and actively working to help other people in our communities does not come naturally. It's not like learning how to walk. These habits need to be taught and they need to be learned. The church can be a great instructor for how to do good in the world. Perhaps the best. We should be the force for good that God desires the church to be in the world, and we should do so by teaching people how to get out and work for the good of others.

Chapter Ten

The Tech Divide

It is no secret that technology has made incredible strides in innovation over the past few decades. From Nintendo to cell phones, multimedia and multi-sensory devices have made their way into most American households, demanding our attention at every waking moment. The world has been opened up to us with the simple glance at a smartphone, while any lull in one's day can be consumed by watching Netflix. We once had to twiddle our thumbs when there was nothing to do, but now we do not have enough time or attention in the day for even half of the ways that our tablets, phones, TV's and computers are made to overstimulate us. At least for some. Others view technology as merely a distraction from the personal, social space that people once occupied. Instead of staying glued to their TV's, some people look longingly at the quiet city streets where children once spent every free hour, missing the days when children used only their imaginations to play with one another. Instead of getting caught up in the excitement of how technology connects us in new ways, they lament how it has eroded what once was good.

On the whole, people from different generations tend to feel differently about the effects of technological innovation on culture and society. Perceptions of changes in how we communicate with one another and entertain ourselves contrast significantly between those who were born in 1955 and those born in 1995. And why wouldn't they be different? In the fifties, operators manually ran phone switchboards, networks broadcast a comparatively few number of shows and news stories, and the U.S. interstate system was just being built. By the nineties, not only had switchboards started to be run by computers, the internet was opening windows to the world through the lens of our personal computers, television channels numbered in the hundreds to broadcast ceaseless programming, and automobile traffic became so congested in several parts of the country that the visionary interstate system cannot handle it. In a very short amount of time, cell phones became the main way many of us connect to one another, with the effect that we can now choose who to talk to virtually anywhere in the world. Those who were born in the fifties had to learn new ways of communicating and operating in a digital world, while those born in the nineties have never known a world without digital devices. Naturally, those who have to relearn what they were taught as kids do not feel as comfortable with how technology has changed the world as those who have grown up immersed in these changes.

Once again, this is nothing new. If we look back through the ages we can see many examples of technological changes which were initially scorned by older generations but embraced by the young of the time. It was not too long ago that people were complaining about kids and their new-fangled rock n' roll music. Before that, I am sure there were many voices complaining about how the young moved west with the railroads, leaving their hometowns behind. Before that, I am sure many people who were established in their European homelands griped about young people and their trending trans-Atlantic travel to the new world. If we go far enough back, I am sure that older generations of cave men complained that younger generations learned how to make fire on their own instead of waiting for the random lightning strike as God intended!

What is unique to our time, though, is how the specific technological innovations have affected who we are together. Technological innovations of the past few decades have resulted in a rapid intergenerational divide. We have become divided in how we communicate, how we form relationships, the places in which we live and interact, and how we get informed. As Christians, technological innovations have driven a wedge between generations in our churches, as well. Young and old have become divided in how we worship, how we study scripture, how we hear the Gospel, and how we share our faith with others. Technological innovation has been a major source for how divided our houses have become, and our houses of worship are no exception.

A significant reason for this divide is that technology has changed the ways in which we learn about the world and how we engage with it. Whereas previous generations were taught by their parents about how to farm, run businesses, work hard, and raise their families, we Millennials have had to teach ourselves how to operate in a digital world. The gradual process of teaching your children or grandchildren what you have learned out of your experience has been usurped by the information age. Though each generation does things a bit differently than the previous ones, the rapid rate of technological invention and innovation in the past few decades has left many parents unable to stay ahead of the curve. Their children have had to fend for themselves. When I learned to use computers I had to look to my peers, not my parents. This is sad, but true.

The effects of the rapid rate of change in the wider world are affecting those in the church, as well. I recently led a Bible study session in which we talked about generational differences and how they are affecting the church. Those in the group ranged in age from their mid-fifties to their mid-eighties. In order to get to a source of why some generations view things differently, I asked the group point-blank, "How many of you taught your children how to use the computer?" As expected, they said, "Our kids had to teach *us*!" I assume that this was the case for most Millennials and parents of Millennials. Technology has moved so fast that it has not only changed the way we communicate and live in the world, it has supplanted parents' ability to teach their children.

Me and mine have had to teach ourselves many things, and our experience of growing up this way has affected how we relate to other generations. For us, age has come to mean something very different than it used to. While age once meant experience, insight, and a wide view of the world, it now means that one is likely behind the times, holding outdated views, and unable to keep up. Sure, this is by no means the whole story of who we are as people, but when we view the world through the lens of technological innovation, youth is privileged and age is disadvantaged. This is in no small part because of the experience we Millennials have had growing up, needing to teach ourselves how to operate in the digital world. When it comes to technology and the fast-paced changing world around us, we received little to no guidance from our parents' generation.

I feel a disclaimer is in order – I am not blaming anyone for anything! I am not saying that one way is right and one way is wrong, or that any generation is doing things better than another. I merely mean to point out that things have shifted dramatically in the technological world and argue that these dramatic shifts have resulted in similar shifts in intergenerational perspectives and communication. Technology has not only divided generations today in terms of how we communicate, spend our free time, and how we work, it has also divided us in how we think, learn and solve problems.

The tech divide between generations has, as often as not, resulted in indignation from older generations towards Millennials. The flipside of having to learn things for ourselves, is that we do not respect the advice of our elders as much as we should. What's worse, many of our ways of thinking and ideas seem uppity and self-involved in comparison with the expectations of other generations who know that their experiences are worthwhile and can teach something to the future. But, a divide has been formed in how we talk to one another, how we learn from one another, and how we respect (or disrespect) one another. For Millennials, good, creative ideas and innovations are key. It does not really matter where or who they come from, a good idea is a good idea. For other generations, especially among Baby Boomers, good ideas are important, but the processes, institutions and experiences which form our ideas are also to be respected. I think that Gen X'ers are somewhere in the middle, but many share frustrations with my generation's attempts to supplant experience in pursuit of new ideas, creativity and self-expression (or whatever you might call it).

The divide that has resulted from technological innovation has combined with institutional failures to make Millennials even more suspicious of what has gone before us. Institutions have done little to impress us in our lifetimes. As we were growing up, the institution of the U.S. government and military responded to the terrorist attacks of September 11, 2001, with dubious intentions and questionable results. Institutions of higher education have bled us dry, forcing most Millennials to have to work our way out of extreme debt upon college graduation (averaging $28,950 by last count[33]) before we can even start thinking about our financial futures. Financial institutions have failed us in greedy and painful ways. Many of us were left unable to find jobs out of college to

[33] "State by State Data | The Institute For College Access and Success." Accessed May 20, 2016. http://ticas.org/posd/map-state-data-2015.

pay off our massive debts because the economy was crippled by the greed of our elders in the Great Recession of 2008, just as we were entering the work force. Sure, my generation has benefitted from growing up in a time when America had decent infrastructure for public education, transportation, and healthcare (to name a few institutions), but we have also come of age with glaring institutional failings that make many, if not most of us, at least a little skeptical.

When we look at the failings of institutions in our lifetimes, combined with technology forcing us to think and learn for ourselves, churches which have long been centers of passing on the faith from one generation to the next suddenly do not look so good. We are institutions that are subject to the same criticisms that all institutions are. In many ways, the church operating as an institution can be clunky, slow moving and resistant to change. In fact, the church as an institution is often more resistant to change than any other institution of our time. The church is costly to support and can often get in the way of helping members to realize their highest ideals. What's perhaps even worse in the minds of Millennials is that the church is an institution which often stifles new ideas. For those of us who grew up having to think for ourselves, a church which does not allow us to do so is not only frustrating, it is abhorrent.

The institutional church can and should be more than an institution. Structures and traditions guide us in our faith lives, but they do not limit us. Though instructions of faith were canonized in the Bible centuries ago, we can still contribute our own words to articulate what God is doing in our lives today. While many hymns and songs are meaningful because they are shared across generations, this fact should not keep us from writing songs of praise to God in our own time and in our own way. Just because Christians have gathered in buildings for a long time now, this fact

94

should not keep us from courageously seeking to share our faith experiences online, in coffee shops, or in other public spaces. The church is an institution which should ground us but not hold us back. We can gather in ways that we have long done, while still working to engage the world in new and creative ways.

All sorts of institutions and technologies have come and gone throughout the history of the church. Unlike the original ipod, the Christian faith is more than a decade and a half old, but this does not mean that the church is outdated. In fact, it means that the church is surprisingly resilient and adaptable, always being renewed by Christ who dwells in it. In the history of Christianity, many other institutions have come and gone. The church has outlived the Roman Empire, feudal European governments, colonial empires, fascism, monarchies, and many dictatorships. The church has persisted through the heyday of trade on the Silk Road, the rise of the mercantile class in cities like Venice, the East India Trading Company, triangular trade across the Atlantic, slavery, and many other businesses which have come and gone all across the world. The church has outlasted legions equipped with shields and spears, British Naval power in the colonial era, and even the use of nuclear weapons in the 20th century. The church is surprisingly resilient and is able to stay current despite the changes and innovations that happen in the world around us.

The church has adapted to changing times before, and I believe that it will again in our time. Though a distracted generation of technophiles is rising up to take up leadership in our society and hopefully our church, this does not mean the end of things which have gone before. A new generation with new ideas means the beginning of a new chapter to be written in the history of the church. This movement is not something to be held at bay or fought against, but embraced.

If Millennials are to stay engaged with the institutional church, we need to be allowed to think through the faith on our own terms. This is our way. For better or for worse, Millennials need to be able to see, discuss, and understand the Christian faith for ourselves if we are to continue in it. We need to understand on our own terms why people go to church and why we ourselves would go to church. We need to be able to recognize how God is real and moving in our own lives if we are to commit to Christianity ourselves. We are a generation who has had to teach ourselves to think and operate in the digital world and the result is that we also need to teach ourselves and learn with one another how to pray, instead of being told to get in line with how people have done it before.

We Millennials also need to be given space to creatively engage, and possibly re-think church on our own terms. Just as we have not had the privilege of learning how to navigate the digital world from our parents, we desire to engage other aspects of our lives on our own, as well. Most of us are not that interested in carrying on traditions just because they were good for people decades ago. We need to be able to see how these traditions are good and meaningful for us in our own lives, in our own time. Opening up opportunities for Millennials to do this means allowing for us to change the church. It is widely accepted that Millennials think and act a little differently from other generations, so it is only natural that if we are accepted in the church, then the church will think and act a little differently, too.

How might the church be changed if Millennials are allowed to contribute to it in our own way? The church will move to have an online presence. People have long existed in physical space together and shared their faith and worship there. As people move to spend time, energy and attention online then the church needs to exist there, too. Since people share their hopes, sorrows, concerns, frustrations online, they should also be able to encounter the Gospel there, as well. Just as people have come to the physical church for centuries with their confessions, their longings, their fears, and their loves, they now bring many of these to Facebook, Twitter, Snapchat, Instagram and a myriad of other online mediums. The church needs to embrace that it should be where the people are because where the people of God live, the Gospel also lives. And wherever the Gospel goes, the church should follow.

It is my hope that if the church can allow itself to be changed by welcoming Millennials for the good and bad we bring, then the technology divide can be bridged. As we work to be church across generations once again, we can reclaim the intergenerational sharing and learning in this generationally divided era. If we look and listen with interest to hear who people are and what they bring to the church, then we will not be divided by our differences, but united by them. If we allow our differences to be a point of bonding, instead of a point of dividing, we will all be better for it.

I serve in a small, rural town in western Montana that is proudly behind the times. Many of my neighbors rejoice that they are not on the cutting edge of innovation, because it allows for us to sit back and enjoy the impeccable mountain vistas which surround us. At the same time, we have to rely on one another to navigate the digital world that has changed around us, because many of us are still getting used to the idea that the world now relies on computers to operate. When I started working in the church, I emailed something to our secretary, Bonnie, and told her to copy and paste it to a new format. She has been using a computer for years and I assumed that she knew how to carry out the basic command of copy and pasting things on the computer. So I said, "Just copy and paste it over to the new format so we can put everything together."

"What's that?" she responded.

97

"What do you mean?" I looked at her quizzically, assuming she was asking a weird question about what I had sent her.

"Ah, whatever you said. Copying and pasting? What is that?"

"What? You don't know how to copy and paste?" I said back, astonished.

"No, I have never done that before."

Bonnie has served as our church secretary for years. She does a wonderful job and has worked with the computer for well over a decade. So, I was floored when, in the year 2014, she had never learned how to copy and paste on the computer. Yet, this little exchange turned out to be a beautiful moment of intergenerational sharing. I quickly showed her how to operate copy and paste commands with the mouse and the keyboard and I have been saving her time ever since.

Around the same time that I was teaching Bonnie to copy and paste, she taught me innovations from another generation. When she takes down notes, I cannot understand a thing that she writes. Initially, I assumed that Bonnie had exceptionally poor penmanship. She wrote in what looked like chicken scratch and the only people I knew growing up who wrote like were people who never learned to write very well. It did not take long before she showed me how wrong I was. She writes in shorthand, a professional writing methodology which many remember well, but one which was replaced by computer keyboards by the time I was growing up. She showed me what I did not know. She was taught to write quickly and professionally when computers were not available and, when she showed me her writing methods, she showed me innovations of her time which I had taken for granted. More importantly, she showed me the creativity of different generations as times gone by.

This kind of intergenerational sharing should happen more often. Bonnie and I stand on different sides of the technological divide. She had to learn to work and communicate before computers and digital devices were a mainstay in offices, schools, and homes. On the other hand, personal computers, faxes, photocopiers, cell phones, etc., have all been around since I was born. She learned to live and operate in a pre-digital world and I have hardly known anything else. It is not only good to share how we in different generations have learned to live and work differently- it is also powerful. When we share in this way, our different places around the tech divide will no longer divide us, they will unite us.

Chapter Eleven

Not so guilty anymore, but feeling smaller than ever

For a long time, the church thrived on moralism. That is, the church was the place where people learned to be good. Parents brought their children to church to not only learn about the Bible and how God loves us, but also to learn how to be good. The church put just as much time, energy and effort into teaching people how to be good citizens of society as it did into actually preaching the Gospel. The church put a huge amount of effort into teaching people not to lie or steal, resist the temptation to cheat on tests, avoid taking the Lord's name in vain, or, God forbid, have sex as a teenager. Whatever peoples' personal beliefs may have been on other doctrines of the church like the doctrine of salvation or the doctrine of the Trinity, a common denominator that kept people coming through the doors of churches in spite of any doubts they may have had, was that the church was the place where good people gathered and where people learned to be good. Moralism in the church was a lowest common denominator between people who really wanted to be in church and those who felt they should be there even though they did not really believe in other things that the church taught.

And you know what? The church loved it! I don't know how many pastors I have met who revel in the days when they could tell people what to do. Pastors, bishops, deacons, church mothers, nuns, priests, and parochial school teachers (to name a few), loved being able to preach at people and tell them how to live their lives. The only thing they loved even more was when parishioners failed to meet expectations so that the church could shame them for their sins. I know many people who have been traumatized by the intense guilt complexes that they received growing up in the church and now live with spiritual, emotional, and moral scars in adulthood, as a result.

Many churches still thrive in this space, self-identifying as places which focus on right and wrong, viewing righteous living as the ultimate purpose that God has for our lives. That is, some churches believe and teach that God values unattainable human perfection more than even Christ's righteousness. Case in point, I write this from western Montana around the Flathead Lake, an area which has many conservative, fundamentalist Christian churches. Outside of many of these churches are billboards on which the Ten Commandments are printed so that drivers can see the laws of God as they pass by and realize just how bad they actually are in God's eyes. Instead of proclaiming messages of grace like, "Jesus was resurrected for you" or "God's grace is for you", our public road space is laden with messages of judgement calling people to repent of sins which they may or may not believe in. This is a misuse of the Ten Commandments. The laws of God have always been intended for the people of God. Attempts to use them to condemn those outside the church is unscriptural and contrary to the will of God as recorded in the law itself. The word of the Lord spoke through the prophets to say that the laws of God were given to the descendants of Abraham in order to *set them apart* from the world, not to judge the world (Exodus 19:5-6, Deuteronomy 7:12, Leviticus 20:26, Jeremiah 11:4).

However churches may self-identify around religious doctrines and whichever messages they choose to focus on, there is common ground that can easily be formed, and has been formed, between the religious world and the secular world through a shared appreciation for moralism. Religious and secular folks both desire for people to be good to one another, so a shared focus on moral messaging is one thing that all can agree on. When talking to non-Christians about the church, especially Millennial non-Christians, they concede that a good thing about the church is that it teaches morality. Those who do not have much or any time for the church at least can get behind it when we teach people to love their neighbors as themselves (Mark 12:31).

Still, the church was better at this in other times than it is now. The church's role in promoting and policing personal morality thrived in a world of "us versus them" thinking. There was a time when we Americans blended together in the melting pot, more or less, to the point at which we could identify a relative 'us' and a relative 'them'. Good guys were in the *us* category while thieves, murderers and other criminals were in the *them* category. Those who worked hard at their jobs were in the *us* category while those who were considered lazy were in the *them* category. Those who had good marriages and families qualified for the *us* category, while those who got divorced or pregnant outside of marriage were in the *them* category. Unfortunately, these categories were never all that accurate, especially since large groups of American minorities (African Americans, American Indians, Asian Americans, Hispanic Americans, etc.) were excluded from ever being in the *us* category, despite being American citizens themselves. Nevertheless, rightly or wrongly, there was a time when the world could more easily be separated into two opposing categories.

I saw an instance of this type of thinking a couple of years ago when I watched the first *Batman* movie with Adam West.[34] At one part in the movie, Batman and

Robin come across a timed bomb that the Joker had set up in the upstairs room of *Ye Olde Benbow Tavern* on a fisherman's wharf. Of course, Batman and Robin had to save the day, so Batman heroically picked up the bomb and ran downstairs to dispose of the bomb. When he reached the first level he ran into a tavern full of drunks who did not know what was going on, just before Batman frantically turned around, headed out the door, comically ran down the wharf for awhile, and then threw the bomb in the harbor from the dock. After the danger was averted, Robin asked Batman, "You risked your life to save that riff raff in the bar?" to which Batman chivalrously responded, "They may be drinkers Robin, but they're also human beings and may be salvaged. I had to!" Though the dialog meant to point at a greater sense of humanity, it ultimately portrayed that Batman was the exception not the norm in letting a pub full of people live. Robin did not think that the idea of killing dozens of people with the Joker's bomb was horrifying, because he did not see their humanity. He saw them as extras at the bar, and assumed others would, too. In Robin's mind, he and Batman were the good guys in the *us* category who did not need to be concerned with the well-being of people in the *them* category, the pub patrons. This movie showed to me, as a Millennial, that the "us vs. them" worldview was alive and well in 1966.

Operating within the *us vs. them* worldview, the church's role in previous decades was to proclaim the good and renounce the bad, taking a stand against the evil in our midst. This dynamic was played out when the church distinguished some people as liars while others were honest, some people as drunkards while others sober, some people as lazy while others hard workers, and some people as untrustworthy while others trustworthy. This kind of thinking cuts the world in two

[34] Martinson, Leslie H. *Batman: The Movie*. Adventure, Comedy, Family, 1966.

on a variety of issues. A threshold was formed from which some are above and worthy of admiration while the rest of the world is below and worthy of reform. Yet, if those below the threshold could not be reformed then they should be judged and condemned. Other language for this worldview is that some are considered to be on the inside while others outside, some make the grade while others don't, and some are worthy but the rest are not. The church thrived on preaching this kind of moralistic messaging, cutting the world apart and placing people into either/or categories, ultimately distinguishing some as good and worthy of God's salvation while others are bad and deserving only of condemnation.

Yet, the world has changed, I believe for the better, so that we see and understand the diversity of those around us more honestly than we used to. I am not speaking just of ethnic and racial diversity, though those are included. The world has changed to help us see and understand that the world does not break down in to two opposing categories (good vs. evil, black vs. white, rich vs. poor), but is made up of several groups and perspectives which at times are opposed to each other while at other moments aligning. Most do not think of the world in the same binary terms that we once did. Maybe this is because of the fall of the Soviet Union and the dismantling of the Iron Curtain which divided the entire world, more or less, along two sides of a massive geopolitical dispute. Maybe this is because of the rise of post-modern thought in which people no longer look to single sources and methods as authorities on what is true and what is false. Maybe there is another reason for the change, but now people see a variety of competing and co-existing "truth" claims which lead one in different directions at the same time, instead of just one way or the other.

Now, instead of viewing people as being on one side of things or the other, more and more of us recognize that people are just people – flawed individuals who make good and bad choices. While some are extremely good and a few are extremely bad, most people are a mix. Views have changed so that people now recognize others as being more than types of people who lie or tell the truth to being people who tell both, the truth and lies. Instead of viewing the world as consisting of drunkards and Teetotalers, people better recognize that there are people who don't drink, some who consume a little once in a while, others who party hard, others who drink alone, and others who are addicted, often to all kinds of substances. Views have changed to be more accommodating and, I would say, honest. People now acknowledge that the world does not consist of some sinners and some saints, but people who are both sinner and saint at the same time.

I am not saying that the forces of evil which existed in our world before have somehow gone away. On the contrary, I believe that evil is as active in our time as much in the present as it ever was. I merely mean to point out that evil is perceived differently than it used to be. From my own vantage point, I would venture to guess that some things are worse than ever. For instance, drug use is trending higher than ever at the moment.[35] Drug use has a firmer hold on people than ever before. What has changed in our time, though, is the view of the drug user. Many, especially Millennials, do not view drug users in absolutist terms. In our minds, not all drug users are alike. The fellow down the street who smokes weed regularly is of much less concern than the meth users a street over. Forces of terror and violence in our world seem as high as ever. School shootings, fundamentalist bombings, genocidal activities of groups like Boko Haram and ISIS are a daily

[35] Abuse, National Institute on Drug. "Nationwide Trends." Accessed May 5, 2016. https://www.drugabuse.gov/publications/drugfacts/nationwide-trends.

feature in the news. Yet, most of the tragic happenings do not translate into guilt over individual sins. I was sixteen on September 11, 2001, and the U.S. response to these terrorist activities played a major role in my formative years. Not once did I believe that God was punishing the United States because of my sinfulness or any other individual sins of American citizens. I, along with others, did however grow up believing that we need to change systems which advocate violence, and improve society on the whole. We did not have guilty consciences when New York was attacked, but we did question whether all of our responses to the violence were done in accordance with God's will.

As a result of these changed worldviews, many seem to have a different sense of personal guilt than used to be commonplace. Since people understand more and more that we, as people, are good and bad at the same time, we are not left with the same sense of personal guilt like used to be taught. We do not have the same guilty consciences which once motivated many to seek the grace of God in the church. People are good and people are bad, usually the same people. Sure, some things are heinously evil like murdering someone or extorting millions of everyday people out of their money, but on the whole many people do not fear hell fire waiting at their door for having told a lie or cheated on a boyfriend.

Meanwhile, at the same time as the generational transition is occurring over how people feel about their personal sins and wrongs, people are now very aware of struggles with things like mental illness, addictions, depression, suicidal thoughts and general feelings of worthlessness. These challenges to human well-being plague members of all generations. These are the experiences of evil in our world that people outside of the church would bring with them and lay at the foot of the cross if they could. What's more, these feelings are especially present among Millennials since we have the

106

highest percentage of suicidal and depressed people in the United States at the moment.[36] Now, perhaps more than ever, people need to hear how God forms, loves and redeems the world through the gift of the Son, Jesus Christ. God sees us differently than many people see themselves and there is a need for the church to encourage the world by reassuring people that they are made in the image of God (Genesis 1), and that they are loved (John 3:16).

Though someone my age may be pretty reluctant to hear you bash on them for having sex as an unmarried person in their twenties, there are plenty of powerful words from God which can speak to the brokenness and emptiness that one's failed relationships have left in their lives. A 26-year-old woman may not have time for Baby Boomers telling her how abortion is murder, but she will likely want to hear that God chose to change the world through the lives of several women who were victimized throughout the Bible. A 24-year-old man probably won't endure people telling him that the reason the world is messed up these days is because people drink too much, but he will probably be moved by a church that wants to honestly walk with him through his struggles with addiction.

Instead of relying on throwing the laws of God at people who don't add up (which is all of us), it is my hope that the church would refocus on boldly declaring the grace filled promises of God. God spoke through the prophet Jeremiah saying, "For surely I know the plans I have for you, says the Lord, plans for your welfare and not for harm, to give you a future with hope" (Jer. 29:11). While the prophet was speaking directly about the ancient Israelites returning from their exile in Babylon, these words reveal powerful truths about the

[36] Abuse, National Institute on Drug. "Nationwide Trends." Accessed May 5, 2016. https://www.drugabuse.gov/publications/drugfacts/nationwide-trends.

nature of God. God is a being who desires that the people of God be taken care of. It is easy to imagine, as many other religions throughout the history of the world have, that God would desire to kick us around. When we mess up, it is easy to fall into the trap of believing that God wants us to get what is coming to us. But this is not the case. Whatever harm we have suffered or evil we have committed, God desires to bring us home and care for us. What's more, God has plans to work for our well-being on our behalf. God is intentional in planning for our welfare and actively cares for us, no matter how bad we've messed up.

The blessed words of the prophets do not stop there. The prophecies of the book of Isaiah look to the future that God is planning with a blessed vision. "He gives power to the faint, and strengthens the powerless. Even youths will faint and be weary, and the young will fall exhausted; but those who wait for the Lord shall renew their strength, they shall mount up with wings like eagles, they shall run and not be weary, they shall walk and not faint" (Isaiah 40:29-31). God desires for us to live beyond the limitations of our lives in this world. God spoke through the prophets to declare that our Creator gives power to the faint and strength to the powerless. God is found in our weakness, but God is not limited to our weakness. The prophets declared that God desires to minister to our brokenness so that we will be able to do all sorts of cool stuff like running without getting tired, walking without fainting, and even soaring through the sky like eagles. I am sure that many of us would settle for being blessed with the ability to find friends who do not betray, jobs that are satisfying and pay livable wages, and faithful partners in our relationships, but the point is well taken. God does not desire for us to be broken, but mended. The Lord does not desire for us to be wounded, but healed.

The greatest evidence that God desires to lead us beyond our brokenness is found in the gift of the Son to the world – Jesus Christ. John 3:16 and following proclaims ever so famously, "For God so loved the *world* that he gave his only Son, so that everyone who believes in him may not perish but may have eternal life. Indeed, God did not send the Son into the world to condemn the world, but in order that the world might be saved through him" (John 3:16-17). God does not desire for only some holy rollers to be saved at the expense of the sinners around them. God does not desire to save only Americans, or Europeans, or Israelites. God came to the earth to save the whole world, that all of us might find redemption in the One who loves us all. This is simply who God is, and we Christians trust in this truth because God acted to make it happen. God does not desire for us to dwell in our brokenness, but acted to save us from it by sending his Son into the world to give us a new dwelling place.

The church is called to proclaim God's love to the whole world, instead of judgment upon everyone for not being good enough. There may have been a time for the church to hammer home individual righteousness, but times have changed. Many of us do not care anymore about the ways the church judges our many and varied sins. We do not feel so guilty for small lies we have told or hearts we have broken, and, even if we do, many do not care what God thinks about these sins. But, people my age have all the time in the world to hear about how God cares for our brokenness. Though we may not always show it, most of us feel as worthless as ever. The Gospel message - that we are all formed and re-formed in the image of God through Christ Jesus - is something that the world cannot give. The Gospel message of God's love for us in our brokenness is something that people in the world still need to hear. A church that is focused on proclaiming the love of God to the brokenhearted, no matter what these people have done, is a church that is doing things right.

While the world has learned to be good on its own (at least good enough), it cannot proclaim the wonderful and mysterious truth that our lives have meaning and worth beyond the here and now, often in spite of it. The simple, profound message that our lives have eternal worth in the eyes of our Creator is a unique, timeless proclamation of the church. As more and more people live life "unchurched", fewer and fewer of us know and trust that our value is in our existence, not in our performance. The Gospel message that we are made worthy through the creative and redemptive love of God is more relevant now than ever. Let us welcome people to church; not to shame them for their sins, but to reassure them that they are loved, especially when they do not feel like it.

Chapter Twelve

Do not worry about tomorrow... let today's worry be enough

In one of my favorite sermons of all time, Jesus' shared the famous words of this chapter title. In the Sermon on the Mount, Jesus instructed us that we should not be filled with worry by comparing our anxieties with birds of the air and lilies that are thrown into the fire. In the middle of his sermon he levied the strong challenge, "And can any of you by worrying add a single hour to your span of life?" (Matthew 6:27). Powerful. Can worrying add even an hour to your life? An opposite outcome is far more likely; we lose hours of our lives by stressing over things that we cannot change. Worry can be toxic, disheartening and very unhealthy. And yet, just as it is common to worry about our own lives, our own financial future, our own well-being, it is easy for Christians to fall into the unhealthy habit of worrying about the life of our churches. For many of us in the church, a rephrasing of Jesus' challenge to us is apt for our time: "Which of you by worrying can add a single hour to the life of your congregation?" Just as with our own lives, if we fill our Christian communities with worry about the future, then we will likely take away from the hours they have to live instead of adding to them.

Christ's instruction against worrying is a prophetic, counter-cultural message in the United States. News outlets achieve higher ratings and profits from getting people worked up over this, that, and the other thing. Businesses are not content to simply meet the needs which already exist in the marketplace so they create new markets by cultivating desires for more and more stuff. Yet, their marketing strategies leave people feeling perpetually lacking. Heck, even weather personalities get in on the action. They bring stories of horrendous weather from all corners of the country into our households to make it seem that the atmosphere is always full of hurricanes, blizzards and tornadoes – all at the same time! Worry sells, and it has a hold on the culture of the United States. Christian churches are no exception.

God does not desire for us to be worrisome people who worship in worry filled communities. Jesus was not the only one in scripture to say "Do not worry", his voice was only one of many. The wise words of the Psalmist say, "Be still and know that I am God" (Ps. 46:10). Be still. Words that calm the soul and provide peace in our lives. The prophet Elijah was called by the voice of the Lord to a mountain where there was a great wind, so strong that it split the mountains themselves and broke rocks apart. Then there was an earthquake followed by a fire – all elements of chaos which would inspire anxiety in the most stout-hearted among us. But God was not in the chaos or the worry. Instead, after all of the chaos swelled around Elijah and went away, there came the "sound of sheer silence" (1 Kings 19:11-12). Elijah found God in the silence, not in the chaos or the worry. Jesus' words are not only holy, they are therapeutic. They are therapeutic for anxious people and therapeutic for an anxious church.

The church is a place that is formed on the Great Commission which calls us to make disciples of all nations (Matt. 28:19-20). The business of making disciples is all about sharing the Good News of Christ; that God came into our world, was born as a man - Jesus of Nazareth - who being fully man and fully God

112

lived, died and was resurrected to save the world from its sins. This is the Good News which we are called to share. We are not called to share anxieties about the future of the church. We are not called to share our worries about where our children will worship or any worries at all about the survival of the body of Christ. Instead, we are to welcome people into the body of Christ by proclaiming that he is risen for the sake of the world.

The Great Commission, the command that we share the Good News with the world, is easily sidetracked when our worries get in the way. Worry has a funny, but pervasive way of taking hold of our focus and misdirecting us. Anxieties about what people will think of us keeps Christians from sharing our faith. We can easily get more focused on what other people do or do not want to hear than what God wants us to say.

Anxieties about the future survival of the church can force us to look inward at our communities instead of looking out to the world around us which is in need of the Gospel. I know this for I have seen it in many times and many places. It is all too easy for some congregations to have meeting after meeting to discuss how to pay for new sound equipment, which curriculum to use or how to pay the pastor, while complaining that people don't come to church like they used to. Many of these same communities have a hard time reaching out, or even discussing the possibility of sharing the Gospel with those who have not heard it. Members of these communities will almost never venture into the world outside the church with the mission of sharing a word of Christian hope. Perhaps these communities fail to reach out because they do not care to do the work of welcoming new people, perhaps they are uncomfortable, perhaps something else. Regardless of the reasons that keep Christian congregations from reaching beyond themselves, anxieties never help.

As with anything, though, many of us worry about the future of the church because we care about it. As a new father, I get overly concerned about every little scratch and scrape that I see on my son. Even though these have been harmless little marks that leave no lasting damage, I still worry and get anxious about his well-being. As a human observer watching *other* kids play, I say that these types of marks and bruises build character and help kids to grow in our world. As a father, I say, "Yep, falls, scratches and bruises definitely do build character, just don't let any of these happen to my boy!" I worry about my son in a unique way because I care about him in a unique way.

The same is true for the church. There is a lot for people who have been a part of congregations for their whole lives to be anxious about when faced with the uncertain future of our Christian communities. There is a lot to worry about and a lot to lose because we care in unique, personal, and powerful ways about the places in which God meets us and encourages us. As people created by God, our religious convictions are important to us. We worry and have anxieties about the future of the church because we care.

Worries over the absence of future generations from our congregations reveal just how much people care about the future of the church. As a pastor, I frequently hear parents and grandparents despair over the fact that their children and grandchildren are absent from our congregation. For these parents, their worry stems from the fact that they have experienced the church to be a life-giving place in which people encounter the good and living God. They love the church and encounter the love of God through the church, so they worry when these loves are not shared by others in their families whom they also love. They are deeply concerned with younger generations' absence from our faith communities and find this trend worrisome. This in turn creates a worry for the future survival of our

Christian communities in general, since many of those who were hoped to carry the church into the future have already left it.

In anxious times such as these, though, it benefits us to remember words from scripture, "There is no fear in love, but perfect love casts out fear" (1 John 4:18). Our love for God casts out our fear for the future. As Christians, we are called to be a non-anxious presence in the world. Our Christian communities are centered by a peace which passes all understanding and are not defined by our worries and anxieties. Instead, the church is centered by the Prince of Peace who overcomes all our concerns. As a church, we are called to be a light for the world, letting God be in control. Our kingdom is one which is "not of this world" (John 18:36), so we should make sure that our worries are not of this world either.

On the other hand, while anxious times can be challenging for our lives of faith, they now provide us with opportunity. Since we are called into faithful communities which are formed by the God of peace, anxious times give us the opportunity to show to the rest of the world the peace which God gives us. There are many things to be anxious about these days. In the United States alone, we are plagued by extreme political division, terrorist activities, violence of all varieties, economic instability, outrageous medical costs - just to name a few of the challenges of our time. But these anxieties, like all things, can be used by God to work for good in the world. All of these are things which can provide us with more than anxiety - they are also ways in which Christ can speak peace into our lives and the lives of our churches. The anxiety-causing elements of life in our times are also opportunities for Christians and Christian communities to show the peace which Christ gives. In anxious times, the rest of the world can see the peace of Christ in his followers as we all face the same or similar upheavals.

Unfortunately, the church has often responded to anxious times by adding more anxiety. I did a Google search for the phrase "What does the future hold for American Christians?" The search was a simple phrase to see what people think about current trends in the church. The search quickly populated a 149 million results, the first page of which included the article titles *How will the Shocking Decline in Christianity Affect the Future of this Nation?*[37], *Does Christianity Have a Future?*[38], and the most positive of the bunch, *No, American Christianity is Not Dead*[39]. A couple of pages into my searching I could not help but open up the blog piece entitled *Are we Finally Witnessing the Death of Christianity in America?* by Zack Hunt.[40] (I actually enjoyed this piece so take a look if you get a chance). I have read many other articles, blogs and letters to the editor about the bleak future of our church, pointing out that it is only getting bleaker. Many seem all too eager to greet anxious times by piling on opinions and predictions that are even *more* worrisome.

[37] "How Will The Shocking Decline Of Christianity In America Affect The Future Of This Nation?" Accessed May 11, 2016. http://endoftheamericandream.com/archives/how-will-the-shocking-decline-of-christianity-in-america-affect-the-future-of-this-nation.

[38] Moss, Candida. "Does Christianity Have a Future?" *The Daily Beast*, April 12, 2015. http://www.thedailybeast.com/articles/2015/04/12/does-christianity-have-a-future.html.

[39] CNN, Ed Stetzer special to. "No, American Christianity Is Not Dead." *CNN*. Accessed May 11, 2016. http://www.cnn.com/2015/05/16/living/christianity-american-dead/index.html.

[40] "Are We Finally Witnessing The Death Of Christianity In America?" *Zack Hunt*, December 7, 2015. http://zackhunt.net/2015/12/07/are-we-finally-witnessing-the-death-of-christianity-in-america/.

But we as a church can and should change our focus, and especially our messaging, about the anxieties that we face. Christian hope has always meant that there is peace and love beyond the terror of our times. We should not settle for preaching things like saying, "there is more doom and gloom around the corner." Instead, our message should always be one along the lines of, "Do not worry, it is all in God's hands and God is good." What's more, even if one does have a view of the future that is laden with Hellfire, then statistics about church membership don't really matter that much. I don't think anyone will be fighting over who's sitting in grandma Susie's pew in the apocalypse! We should not worry just to worry, and, if we are going to get worked up about stuff, let's get worked up about things that are more important than a few statistics.

Finally, as a Millennial, I must give a final plea in this matter. Our generation has inherited enough anxieties! We are plagued with massive student debt loads, came of age in the housing crisis of the Great Recession making it seem unlikely that we will ever be home owners ourselves, and have inherited an increasing wage disparity between rich and poor which severely threatens the future of the middle class. We have inherited all of these amidst many other negative, anxiety inducing aspects of the future we are living into. Don't make us anxious about the future of the church, too! Sure, like anything else, we have a role in church decline. Yet, like most other things we are not the only cause, so do not pin all of your anxieties on Millennials. We are not the only cause of these anxieties within the church, nor are we the only solution.

Chapter Thirteen

Growing up into church

Many people my age who were forced by their parents to attend church when they were young, often against their will. Most of them were never really given the opportunity to claim their faith on their own terms. This experience formed their relationship to church – what their parents made them do when they were young. As they have grown older, they have stopped going to church for what they feel are the same reasons that they no longer ask the teacher's permission to go to the bathroom and no longer live in fear of the timeout corner. Their church attendance amounted to no more than a parental requirement which they now, as adults, have grown out of.

In a way, this is nothing new. For generations parents have had to push their kids to do chores, eat breakfast with the family, go to school, and do almost anything worthwhile. Children do not always know what is best for them and they do not form many good habits unless they have a mother, father or some other adult telling them what to do and what not to do. For whatever reason, God made most children just a little bratty and leaves it up to us parents to figure out what to do about that.

In the same vein, parents have had to drag their kids to church when they are not willing to go. Parents have to make many choices about what is best for their child and enforce the good, often against staunch resistance. My son, Otto, is only eleven months old, but I have already had to fight him to make sure he is strapped into his car seat, eats pureed vegetables, and goes to sleep when he needs it. I am sure in a few years he will need me to force him to get out of bed to make it to school on time, otherwise that will never happen. I will probably also need to force him to keep his hands to himself and avoid giving other kids bloody noses. He will just not be able to resist on his own. Raising kids in the church has, for many families in many generations, been treated much the same as mandatory school attendance, household chores, or fights on the playground. Even though children may want to do one thing, the parent or adult has to see the better way, make choices for the child, and encourage or even force those choices one way or another.

For many families, including mine, going to church was considered a good thing that kids just had to do. For a long time, it was assumed that families just should go to church, and parents felt that they just had to make sure their children got out of bed on time to do so, even if they were not willing on their own. Makes sense right? For all the reasons I just listed, it is all but expected that church would be a part of good family life since we believe that Christ is found in the church and faith in Christ is a good thing.

But, at least in the United States, something has been changing for a while and now those changes are finally taking center stage. People have many more choices than they ever have had about how to spend their time. This also means that we have more freedom to resent things that were forced on us when we were young. In a world of choice, freedom valued as essential while any sense of compulsion is scorned. I imagine I might have made a few readers cringe a moment ago when I said, "Parents have to make choices about what is good for their child and enforce the good" because that is not how many people want to live or raise their children anymore. The world has changed, and the ability to make choices about what we want out of our increasingly diverse world is part of that change – beginning from a very young age. I am not saying that this is right or wrong, but I am saying that the world has changed and part of the change involves many Millennials resenting the fact that their parents dragged them to church when they were growing up. This resentment is resulting in them staying away from the church now that we are adults.

I imagine other readers are cringing when they think about the effect of generational differences on the church. I have heard all too often from older church goers, something along the lines of, "My parents dragged me to church when I was young, but when I grew up I knew that it was a good thing for me to attend church on my own. I don't understand why this generation won't grow up and start coming to church like we did!" Maybe I'm not getting this sentiment exactly right, but I imagine it is familiar to many of you. A generational pattern formed over time in which older generations raised their young with expectations that it is good to do certain things like attend church. Parents were to teach certain values, expectations and disciplines to their children and when the children grew up they were more or less expected to follow suit. When they became adults themselves, the expectation was that they maintain similar practices and values that their parents did.

The generational divide that has risen with changes in our world has affected the idea of "growing up", so that it means something very different for younger adults than it did for previous generations. While for older generations growing up meant not only going to college but also getting a job, starting a family, purchasing a house, and, hopefully, going to church, for younger adults growing up means a lot of different things. For us, growing up means spending our time in jobs that provide fulfillment as well as income (the two are not synonymous). Growing up means paying off student loans which takes most college graduates at least ten years, if not twenty or thirty, while considering how to take out mortgage debt on top of student debt somewhere in the middle of it all. For many my age, growing up means figuring out who we are and who we will become before starting a family. Many of us work to figure our own lives out while simultaneously figuring out who to spend the rest of our lives with. Our generation has grown up in households which suffered the highest rates of divorce in our country's history, and many of us seem to have commitment issues, as a result.[41] Unfortunately for the church, my generation also seems to think that growing up means growing out of church. Just as things have changed in the business world, the world of media and information, the world of family life, and many other aspects of society, peoples' relationship to the church has changed, too. Growing up means something very different than it used to, especially for the church.

What does growing out of church mean? From a cynical point of view, it means that Christianity is the stuff of children, much like fairy tales or the belief in Santa Claus and the Tooth Fairy. Like these imaginary tales, which are considered suitable for children to believe but not adults, this cynical view of Christianity looks at our religion as nothing more than false stories for childhood imaginations. When one grows to adulthood, mature reason dictates that the cynic put away any Christian belief as false. There are many in this day and age who have this strongly cynical view of Christianity. Shows like South Park and Family Guy often make jokes comparing Jesus to other fictional characters. In other subtle and conspicuous ways,

---

[41] https://www.washingtonpost.com/news/wonk/wp/2015/06/23/144-years-of-marriage-and-divorce-in-the-united-states-in-one-chart/ (Accessed April 6, 2016).

Hollywood cinema casts doubts about the reality of Christ through many movies and shows. It is easy now to be completely and wholly cynical about any and all aspects of Christianity, and difficult to believe in the face of such criticism.

Yet, it is my experience that most people who have "grown out" of church do not hold such extremely cynical views. Most peers my age who have told me that they have grown out of the church speak of a general ambivalence about all religious matters. Sure, they do not believe in the Christian message strong enough to make it to worship on Sunday mornings, but the fact that they do not come to church does not necessarily mean that they are not Christian. In fact, there are many non-church goers that I have met who self-identify as Christian. Though they do not come to church or hear the Gospel proclaimed weekly, they still believe in the Christ who is the foundation of the church.

So what have they grown out of? Many Millennials have grown out of the judgmentalism of the church. That is, we are tired of other people trying to determine what are the right ways for us live and act, and even more tired of people trying to make us feel guilty when we do not live up to their standards. When the church thrived on its own moralism and place at the center of society, it also served as a center for judgment against those who fell outside of the norms. There is wide spread perception these days that churches are no longer communities of patient, peace loving people who advocate and care for the poor. Outsiders' perceptions have changed, believing that the church is full of hypocrites who preach about God's love but turn around and use it as a weapon to point out the unrighteousness of those who do not meet God's standards. Millennials are growing up and out of this kind of judgmentalism, wanting to avoid being judged themselves and wanting no part of communities which perpetuate judgments against others.

We have also grown out of the idea of going to church just because it is a good thing to do. There are lots of good things to do! Now, more than ever before, there is a plethora of non-profits people can volunteer for, causes which one can give to, and interest groups one can join. Long gone are the days which the church was the one and only place in the community where one could go for counseling, family activities, education, hospital services, and food assistance. The organizations and programs which fulfill these functions in society are more numerous now than ever before. One does not need to go to church to be good anymore and many Millennials have grown out of assumptions that church attendance is an essential part of living a good life.

We have grown out of the idea of the church as an authority figure and guide to the good, an institution we should be afraid of frowning on us. If the church cannot exist except as an institution of authority which brings people to heel, relying on their support without concern for their experience in the pews, then the future is pretty bleak. On the whole, Millennials, at least most that I know, have no time for religious figures telling us what to do, and even less time for people standing around in judgment of us.

Yet, we have grown *into* many things, as well. People my age have a rich appreciation for identity. Church communities that can articulate who they are and what their mission is to those inside and outside the congregation might do well with Millennials. This can be a challenge for many established, mainline congregations. Anthony B. Robinson recently published an article in *The Christian Century* in which he put the problem this way: "Since many mainline churches have long assumed a culture of churchgoing, they are often especially challenged when it comes to articulating what it is they are selling. They tend to assume people should want what the church has to offer, even if none of them can quite say what that is."[42] Many mainline members of mainline congregations are not good at articulating who they are as a church or what they believe because we have long relied on the assumption that people should just want to go to church. While this assumption has eroded rapidly around us in the wider world and culture, it has also given way to an opportunity for us to do some soul searching and claim who we are as Christian communities. If we are able to communicate clearly who we are together, I believe that the church will have a surprisingly receptive crowd amongst Millennials.

Another thing that Millennials have grown *into* is a desire to be a part of creative communities which actively envision and re-envision who they are and what they do. I do not know how many friends and family members my age have joined church plants, church starts and emerging communities, I have simply lost count. It seems like everybody my age who is going to church is choosing one startup or another (except me of course). Why is this? I am sure there are many and varied reasons why people choose to join churches that are just getting their feet wet as opposed to churches which are drenched in history and tradition. One major reason, though, is that church plants and church starts allow, encourage and even require members to actively participate in the life of the church in new and creative ways. Established congregations, especially mainline congregations, have a tendency to actively discourage creative participation amongst members, preferring the status quo of how things have been done before. Instead of allowing people to be themselves in the middle of a worshipping community, established congregations have a way of trying to get people to keep doing things the

---

[42] Robinson, Anthony B., "What's your passion?", *The Christian Century*, April 27, 2016, p.11.

way they have been done before. Church starts, on the other hand, do not know who they will be yet, and allow for members to find themselves in the midst of a community that is also trying to find itself.

Established congregations do not need to hide behind their history or what is considered status quo amongst the membership. The tendency of established congregations to stifle the creative engagement and faith seeking of newcomers does not have to be the norm. Established congregations can allow for creative change if they open up opportunities for people to do new things and try out new ideas within the context of the wider established community. For example, if there is an event like a church bazaar, bake sale, or anything else that has worked well in the past, but no longer attracts participation from younger members, a church open to creative energy will allow events like these to end. This frees the community from obligations to burdensome activities that no longer hold interest, and free up time and resources for people to think about new things that the church could start doing. Does your church have committees that nobody wants to join, but have been together for longer than you can remember? Do some soul-searching and let these committees be subject to overhaul by those who do not currently find them appealing. There is no magic formula for change that will attract Millennials into our churches, but one thing I know which certainly drives us away from congregations is the inability of churches to allow for creative change by younger members. We do not want to simply carry on the traditions of what has been done before, and established churches who only know how to think and act this way end up driving the few members of my generation who might join them to look for other churches or start their own.

All this being said, none of us can grow out of our need for the love and mercy that is found in Christ alone. For all the ways we may wish it were so, we

Millennials are not God. We need Christ in our lives the same as anybody else. We need to be re-affirmed that we are made by a loving God who cares for us, who saved us by the Christ who gave his life to make us whole, and who divinely comforts us by the Holy Spirit. For all that has changed in the world around us, our need to relate to our God who loves us has not. Therefore, those of us in established, mainline congregations should allow ourselves to be changed by a changed world so that the light of God may continue to be proclaimed through our communities of faith. God can and does dwell in the changes to our world, and we should open ourselves to recognize God in these changes.

Chapter Fourteen

Wrestling with the legacy of Christendom

Christendom is the idea of the Christian society and the Christian state. In other words, Christendom is the idea of the Christian nation and Christian empire. The idea of Christendom prevailed, more or less, in western Europe during much of the 2nd millennium A.D. From small feudal kingdoms crawling out of the dark ages to the beginnings of imperial, colonial Christian empires, the only thing that seemed to form a common bond between many European countries for hundreds of years was that Christianity was the state religion. Kings were banded together under the authority of St. Peter's successor in Rome up through the Protestant Reformation. Then, for centuries after the Reformation until recently, Europe has still been a continent of Christian kings, prime ministers, and citizens. For centuries, European states have been Christian countries. Though these peoples and countries have warred over many things throughout many generations, a guiding identity for all was that most of their citizens were baptized and believed that Christ rules over all.

Much of contemporary pushback against Christianity, I would argue, overlaps with pushback against the idea of Christendom. Many people in our time equate the idea of the medieval Christian king and the medieval Christian priest, and use them as examples by which to judge present day Christians. They do not distinguish between medieval kings and priests who wielded the power and authority of the church over the common person, and the rich, personal faith experiences of individuals in our contemporary world. Many outside the church fail to understand the subtle contrast between the monk who lives his life committed to daily prayer, the revivalist who preaches conversion experience in the American south, the Ethiopian convert who has come to faith in the last decade, or the working mother who comes to church on her one day off because she believes that there is something powerful that happens on a Sunday morning. All of these varied, individual faith experiences, as well as larger understandings of what Christianity is as a religion, often get judged on the basis of the history of Christendom in Europe and its negative impacts on the world.

Some of this push back is warranted, especially when one considers the very long history in the church of conflating the salvation which God offers and the authority of the church. Christianity started out on the margins, but it did not stay that way for long. The church began after Jesus was crucified, a death which was reserved for political agitators. The Messiah, the foundation of the church, was not part of the Roman state but stood against it. His disciples are believed to have had a high propensity for death, with ten being martyred, one committing suicide or tripping and falling to his death depending on which account you prefer (see Matt. 27:5 and Acts 1:18), with only one living to a natural death.[43] In the first two centuries of Christian history, Christians were on the margins of the Roman world, facing many periods of substantial persecution and martyrdom. Though there is some debate about how bad these persecutions actually were, it is clear

---

[43] http://www.christianity.com/church/church-history/timeline/1-300/whatever-happened-to-the-twelve-apostles-11629558.html Accessed January 19, 2016.

that Christianity was not at the center of Roman society in its early years.

Christianity's role in the Roman world changed rather quickly with its rapid growth, the conversion of the Emperor Constantine, and the act of Emperor Theodosius II making Christianity the official religion of the empire. Being at first illegal and subject to widespread persecution throughout the empire, Christianity was soon adopted at the highest levels of government, military, and society. The religion that had started out on the margins and in the backwaters of the empire moved to take center stage, still reigning at the center of the city of Rome to this day.

Accompanying the movement of Christianity to the center of the Roman world was the idea of the Christian society. In Christianity's beginning, there was not even the possibility of thinking about the whole, the majority, or even a significant portion of society being Christian. However, when Christianity was adopted by the empire there was no way to keep from seeing society and Christianity together. The state now overlapped with the church, and has done so in the western world until relatively recently. This means that the church was complicit and active in many actions that the state perpetrated or, at the very least, lost the credibility of its voice as a countercultural institution.

As with any state religion, the idea of Christendom required religious coercion by the state. For a nation to truly be a "Christian nation" there had to be at the very least a status quo of Christianity and, as was most common in Christendom, Christian standards enforced by the government. In the Christian countries that composed the nation states of Christendom, people were forced to pay money in support of the church. This is still the case in many European countries. Unlike American congregations which are supported through voluntary, free-will tithing on the part of congregants, European Christianity and Christendom was supported through taxation. For them, being a Christian nation meant that the citizens of that nation were forced to support the church, much as people in any country are forced to pay their taxes. Along with this, it was expected that people attend church at least once a year, get their children baptized and confirmed, get married in the Christian church and have funeral ceremonies conducted by the priest or pastor with a Christian burial.

Now, all of these things are probably not so bad. Sure, many people don't want to be taxed at all, for anything, so being forced to pay to support churches that they do not really attend is not a choice many would make on their own. Yet, is it really so bad to be married and buried at a church and only a church? Perhaps, but even many agnostics and atheists might agree that this is not the biggest problem with the idea of Christendom. If Christendom were just about rituals and rites of passage, then I do not think that it would be all that disagreeable to most, even to those who do not believe in God or in Jesus Christ.

The real challenge which people have with the idea of Christendom and its legacy is its history of coercion - that is, the history of forcing others to convert to Christianity or die. While it was once commonplace in the Western world to believe that one must accept the tenets of Christianity or face exclusion, imprisonment or death, this history that is a significant part of the legacy of Christendom is now being widely scrutinized in Europe and the United States. If Christianity relies upon forcing people to believe what they do not believe, then it is hard to say that Christianity has much of a place in free societies and free countries. Yet, the idea of Christendom necessarily relies on coercion since it has never been the case, even when Europe most resembled Christendom, that everyone in every Christian country freely accepted the teachings of the church and the central tenets of Christianity.

While the adoption of Christianity by the Roman Empire was good for the authority of the church and its leaders, as well as the stability of the church in Europe, its central place of authority is also being called into question in our present day and age. Most significantly, Millennials are pushing back against the idea that salvation is found in the church and in the church alone. Even among those who claim to be Christian, many question whether salvation is found only in the church. I have heard a lot of Christians say, "I am not religious but I accept Jesus as my personal savior." This is kind of a ridiculous thing to say because acceptance of Christ is a religious belief and action. Still, behind this statement is a sentiment that the church should be paying attention to. People desire to love, praise and worship God but struggle to find God and Jesus Christ in the institutional church. Even though many people still want to be Christian, at least in the United States, more and more of them do not want to go to church.

On the other end, the response from many within the church, myself included at times, seems to be formed by the long history of believing that Christ and Christ's salvation belong to the church alone. It is hard for many of us to conceive of Christ thriving outside of the church. After all, how would Christianity survive if not for the collective worship, teaching, preaching and sacramental living of Christian communities? It is all well and good to say you find Jesus on the mountain or wherever else, but many of us who still attend church believe that Jesus is found in the church and primarily the church. While many on the outside struggle to see Christ in it at all, many of us who are still in the church struggle to see Christ without it. This is also part of the legacy of Christendom.

The idea that Christ is found in the church alone grew through the adoption of Christianity as the religion of the empire, was supported as churches came to the center of public life in the dark ages of Europe after the fall of Rome in western Europe,[44] and was perpetuated through the rule of Charlemagne who spread the Christian faith by conquering nations with the sword.[45] As the world became globalized with sea trade between east and west as well as trans-Atlantic voyages beginning with Columbus's fateful journey in 1492, Christianization was a justification for Western trade practices and colonization of foreign nations which often turned out to be brutal and oppressive. It was believed that any encounter which non-Christian peoples around the globe had with Europeans was good because it was an encounter with Christianity, and, therefore, a gateway to encountering Christ himself. Even though millions were killed, oppressed and enslaved as a result, Christianity provided the justification for European countries to spread culture and commerce throughout the world, by any means necessary. Christianity and European society became so intertwined that many Europeans believed that it was good for them to enslave foreign peoples because that way the enslaved could receive Christ's salvation through the instruction of their Christian overlords. In the settlement of the American west, for instance, though church and state were officially separate, the presence of missionaries on the frontier made for a convenient excuse to call in the U.S. Calvary against the American Indian nations who dwelt in North America long before the name of Christ was spoken on the continent.

There have been far too many instances when Christian societies have not acted very Christ-like, and insofar as the institutional church still resembles these

---

[44] Irvin, Dale T., and Scott W. Sunquist. *History of the World Christian Movement: Earliest Christianity to 1453*. 8/16/01 edition. Maryknoll, N.Y: Orbis Books, 2001.

[45] Wilson, Derek. *Charlemagne*. Vintage, 2007.

un-Christ like unions of church and state, doubts will abound whether salvation is found in the church at all, let alone whether it is found only in the church. Worries and arguments that people should come to church in order to receive salvation are now greeted with much greater suspicion and criticism than they used to be. The problem this poses for intergenerational dialogue is that many generations of church goers have been taught that those who are not right with the church are not right with God. Yet, younger adults struggle with how one can be good and still part of an institution that has sinned so egregiously and unrepentantly in the past.

Today, the legacy of Christendom is still active because it has formed cultural norms of expecting people to be Christian, regardless of how they may personally feel about the faith. I am a Christian and, as a Christian, I believe that Jesus Christ is "the Way, the Truth and the Life" (John 14:6). Being Christians who believe that we are saved in Jesus Christ, it seems only natural to desire that all of our friends and neighbors be Christians, too. As we believe and have certainty through faith that we are saved in the blood of Christ, we are more likely assured of our friends' and families' salvation if we share our Christian faith with them.

Yet, Christianity should never have involved forcing people into the faith because the call to discipleship was always meant to be an open, free invitation. Even Jesus Christ himself did not coerce a single individual into the faith. How did Jesus call his disciples? By command or by invitation? Invitation. Period. He said, "Come, follow me" over and over again as he called disciple after disciple. This was how Jesus called his disciples in the gospels. He did not threaten anyone with fears of Hell or curses of death. He did not force his way by having any cronies with clubs and swords make people join him or else. He did not try to court power to his cause or pay people off. A simple, confident invitation was all that he offered.

When Jesus called Simon (Peter) and his brother he said, "Follow me, and I will make you fish for people" (Matt. 4:19). Follow me. When Jesus saw two other fishermen – soon to be disciples – he simply called them and they followed him (Matt. 4:21-22). He called, they followed. In perhaps one of the most challenging call stories in the gospel of Matthew, a soon to be disciple said to him, "Lord, first let me go and bury my father" (Matthew 8:21). A simple, good request. Let me honor my father by burying him. But Jesus' call was the same, "Follow me, and let the dead bury their own dead" (Matt. 8:22). Follow me. Even when facing shame before the family and neglecting his duties as a son, Jesus did not coerce his disciple to follow him. He repeated the simple call, follow me, and then explained that those who have hope for new life do not need to put their life on hold mourning losses. The text does not tell us if the disciple in question actually followed or not, but it seems likely that he did. Regardless, Jesus did not say, "Follow me or else you are going to Hell!" He did not say, "Follow me or you will not be saved!" Nor did he coerce people with reward saying, "Follow me and you will be rich and powerful in the Kingdom of God!" Or, "Follow me, and I will make sure that your parents and children have eternal life." The call was always, simply, "Follow me."

The call to discipleship did not even change when calling one that Jesus should have been at odds with – a tax collector. Tax collectors in Jesus' day were seen as extortionists and betrayers of their own people. They were deputized by the Roman empire to collect taxes by force from their own people. They would show up at people's houses with soldiers at their backs to coerce them to pay their taxes to Rome, collect the amount owed to the empire, then collect extra for their own payment. As you can imagine, the temptation to overcharge was strong and many tax collectors took far more than necessary in order to make themselves rich at the expense of their own people. When Jesus called Matthew, one such tax collector and betrayer of his people, we might expect that he would say something to the effect of, "Follow me so that I can save you from your evil deeds," or "Pay everyone back any money that you took so that you can be good enough to be my disciple." But Jesus' call to Matthew remained the same. "Follow me" (Matt. 9:9). Uncoerced, Matthew responded to the invitation and followed Jesus.

Likewise, we are called to invite others to be disciples of Christ by simply sharing the call for others to freely follow, not forcing anyone. Jesus commanded us in the Great Commission to go out to the whole world and follow his example of making disciples. "Go therefore and make disciples of all nations, baptizing them in the name of the Father and of the Son and of the Holy Spirit, and teaching them to obey everything that I have commanded you" (Matt. 28:19-20). Jesus' final words in the gospel of Matthew were that we reach out to the whole world by inviting others to follow him and become his disciples. We too, are called to *invite* people to follow Jesus, not force them to do so with threats of Hell fire, or concerns over the dissolution of the morals of society. We are called to invite people to be disciples of Jesus in the same way that he called the original disciples – offering a free invitation which was taken up by many and freely denied by others.

The very notion of Christendom rubs up against a lot of what Jesus said in the gospels. At times he was very anti-imperial like when he said to Pontius Pilate in the book of John, "You would have no power over me unless it had been given you from above..." (John 19:11). By saying this he declared that the authority of Pontius Pilate, the representative of the empire in that area, was not secured by war, economic superiority, or anything of the sort, but could be given and taken away in an instant by God the Father. At other times, though,

Jesus spoke more moderately about the co-existence of the church and state. When questioned on whether it was lawful or not to pay taxes to Rome, thereby supporting the empire, Jesus responded by pointing to the image of the emperor printed on the Roman currency and saying, "Give therefore to the emperor the things that are the emperor's, and to God the things that are God's" (Matt. 22:21). With statements like this it seems that limited connection between Christianity and the empire seems to have been permitted. At the same time, Jesus clearly drew a line between the church and the state, saying that paying taxes to the emperor had nothing to do with the faith of the people.

With the adoption of Christianity as the religion of the empire came the notion that one *should* be a Christian to be a good member of society. The emperor and many aristocrats were expected to be Christian. State ceremonies were conducted by Christian priests and Christianity became the status quo for the masses of citizens within the empire. With this new religion of the state came the expectation that upstanding citizens *should* be Christian. This changed how people came to the faith in two distinct and lasting ways which still affect our religion and society today. The first effect is that many people converted who probably did not actually believe in Christ, they just felt they had to. This muddled the once fervent Christian communities of worshippers who previously gathered under the threat of imprisonment and death. Christianity's adoption as the religion of the empire made the church a place where it was a good, acceptable and proper to gather. This change in dynamic has made it more of a challenge for the church to encourage fervid engagement amongst all of our members, basically ever since.

The second way that we are still wrestling with the legacy of Christendom today is the idea that one *must* be a Christian and be *forced* to be one even if they do not want to be. This obligatory culture of church attendance is not appealing to Millennials. We do not want to be forced into anything, and will resist any institution that tries to talk about membership in compulsory terms. This response is not limited to Millennials. I have witnessed resistance from people of any age group, young or old, against the old idea that one must simply go to church. Disciplining oneself to attend church regularly is a great practice, but forcing personal disciplines on others is no good. People are aware of this now more than ever.

There are many reasons that one might want to continue imposing the faith on others. Christian faith provides comfort in times of grief, courage in times of adversity, humility in periods of success, patience in times of trial...the list goes on. Being able to prayerfully bring concerns to God in times of trouble and being renewed by the Word of God is life giving. Yet, faith takes root and is at its richest if it is willfully and intentionally lived into. If the believer is able to daily and voluntarily call on God's name un-coerced, then faith that is life giving is allowed to bloom on its own. If one is a Christian simply because he or she is required to be, then his or her faith may easily topple or simply be left behind when requirements change.

The problem of our time may not be that the church is failing to do things well, or that the Christian faith does not really work for people anymore. The problem of our time may be that societal expectations around church attendance have changed, while the long cultivated reason for attending church has been solely a sense of obligation. Feeling no obligation to attend, many people these days simply will not choose to attend on their own. If the only reason we know to attend church is because of requirements imposed on us, then how would we make it through the church doors when expectations to do so are gone? Would one really expect people to pay money and put in a lot of hours to complete driver's education if it was not required? Sure, some people probably would, but many would not. Would we expect people to pay fines or obey speed limits if they were not enforced? Would we expect many people to pay taxes if we did not have to? Perhaps some people would... I believe that the western church, riding in the wake of the idea of Christendom, has relied on people participating in church life out of a sense of duty for too long, which is resulting in the church's current decline. For too long the church, especially mainline churches, have just expected people to come through our doors. But these expectations have done damage to the ability of many young adults to claim the faith for themselves. When church attendance is relegated to the realm of *duty* and *requirement*, as they long have been, then many people are robbed of the opportunity to attend out of their own free will.

What's more, by relying on cultural expectations that people come to church out of a sense of duty or requirement, the church has robbed itself time and again of the wonderful opportunity to practice Christ-like evangelism and invite people to encounter the Gospel for themselves. Jesus invited his followers, un-coerced, to follow him in order to hear the Good News. The church that relies solely upon people coming to them, instead of doing the work of inviting, is not following Christ's example. Jesus Christ made disciples by saying to them, "Follow me", then letting those he called to respond freely and faithfully. Many American congregations, however, have too long relied upon people feeling guilty for not attending. Or worse, they inspire fear in people that if they do not attend church, than Jesus will not forgive them of their sins and they will be subject to the judgement of God. A far cry from the open, *free* invitation to follow Christ.

I recently talked about something that I was reading with a young member of our church named Gracie. Gracie is in the sixth grade and has a keen mind for many things, so I did not hold back from discussing something that might be challenging to younger minds. In our conversation I said, "I have been reading Icelandic sagas recently and one was about an old Norwegian king named Olaf. You are Norwegian, right?"

"Yes," she responded with keener interest.

"Well," I said, "King Olaf was a refugee as a child on the eastern part of the Baltic sea where he was raised Christian, even though he grew up in the age of Vikings when many of his people were not Christian. Part of how he came back to Norway and took back power was that he would conquer villages and then force the people to be baptized and become Christian."

"Hmm..." she said, "I don't really think that is right. I mean, I am glad that they became Christians but I don't think it was good to force people to be baptized."

Even as a sixth grader, Gracie's 21st century sensibilities no longer accept the idea of coercing people into the faith. Already at a young age, she rejected the idea of a Christian nation in which citizenship in the Christian society meant forcefully routing out any dissent against the faith. I believe that Gracie speaks not only for her budding generation but my generation of Millennials, as well.

Chapter Fifteen

Desperate times call for desperate evangelism

A colleague of mine, Rev. Dan Heskett, shared that back in the 1990's he participated in all sorts of seminars and conferences which focused on the changes in the world around the church. Trends were coming down the pipeline which meant the world was changing as things rapidly moving from the real world to the digital world. Young people were migrating from having face to face conversations to spending hours communicating via instant messenger. Steady commitments that people used to have towards institutions like the church were already waning and the church started feeling the crunch. At the same time, within the church, there were heavy worship wars going on which pitted Christians against one another over visions of the right way to worship. Evangelicalism continued to bloom at an increasing rate while mainline churches struggled to articulate why congregational models, liturgical worship, and full-time, well-educated clergy were the right formulas for Christian churches in contemporary America. Indeed, it was the first time many churches and pastors were thoroughly and critically questioned on why we do what we do. Most of us never had to put up that kind of defense before.

So, my colleague said, "Back in the '90's I participated in all sorts of trainings and conferences about trends in the world and what to expect from the future. The theme of every one of them was, 'The world is about to change'. It is clear now that that the world *has* changed."

The world has changed. A simple but powerful truth that we need to accept. We can and do react to this reality in different ways. I have argued through the course of this book for what I believe are better ways to react to the changes that we Millennials have brought and will continue to bring to the faith communities we are a part of. On the other hand, many in the church react to the changed world around us in ways that are not good or beneficial. Instead of embracing the creative change that me and mine desire to contribute to the church, we are stifled in many ways and told to respect the wisdom and traditions of our elders. Instead of thinking collectively about how to live into the future together, the young are often and widely blamed for failing the expectations of older generations. Instead of letting the challenges our time unite us by working together to find a way forward, we have too long let them be causes for division. We have done this by blaming younger generations as the only cause for the problems and, therefore, the only generations who need to find solutions to them.

I suppose this is nothing new. The image of the grumpy old church goer is not exactly a ground-breaking one. I am sure everyone who has been involved in a church community can remember being scolded as a child or, even better, seeing one of your friends get in trouble when you were young. Whether it was five years ago or seventy-five years ago, generational differences between young and old have long resulted in tensions and disagreements about best practices, how to behave, what is the right way to worship, etc. It has always been difficult for younger generations and older generations to see eye to eye, and to live as Christians in community with one another.

What is unique to our time, though, is that Millennials are not putting up with the unwillingness of our elders to allow a place for us in the future of the church. We are a creative bunch who desire to actively engage with the world around us. While it is true many of us Millennials are increasingly faithless, there are still many of us who continue to live as faithful Christians. Yet, even though many of us continue in the Christian faith on our own, the faithful who remain committed to Christ are not going to stick around in congregations that harp on us for our differences. Nor will Millennials wait around for direction from other generations who grew up in very different times and in very different worlds. When it comes to intergenerational pushing and shoving, most of my peers will not tolerate judgments, criticisms, and blame from older generations within Christian communities. Instead of abiding the criticisms of our elders, many Millennials will leave multi-generational church communities and join age segregated church starts where we don't have to deal with criticisms about how everything we are doing is wrong. Worse yet, most Millennials will deal with generational disputes by leaving the church completely behind.

But, this is an assessment of people within the church. Most Millennials are not only unchurched, we really have a very limited understanding of what the church is. Many in my generation were raised to prioritize sporting events, fishing trips, overnights with friends, sleeping in, or playing video games over going to church regularly. For those of us who did go to church, the majority of us came of age in a time when Christian rhetoric and messaging was wonderfully passionate and inspiring about our personal relationships to the divine, but at the same time painfully narrow and one-dimensional. These trends have resulted in a generational apathy toward participation in Christian community as other interests have crowded out the space that Christianity once occupied in our world. Many of us have been lured into viewing the church and Christianity as primarily and only about understanding the message of Jesus and living in a more or less Christian, Biblical way. This simplified, dare I say shallow, understanding of Christianity can now be lived out from our couch while watching a Joel Oesteen sermon on TV once a month or from our smartphones on which we find a myriad of Christian podcasts to accompany us on morning workouts and commutes. The Christian church has been out-prioritized and out-messaged, leaving many in my generation with little motivation or reason to make it to a physical church building on Sundays.

In response, the church needs to bear witness to itself in contemporary America. We cannot expect people to just come through the church doors any longer. We need to articulate why the church matters as a bearer of Christ to the world in our modern era. We need to help people see that Christianity is about more than just understanding the Jesus story. The church needs to rise up and bear witness to its multi-dimensional nature as the instrument through which the Holy Spirit moves to bring people to faith in Jesus Christ, feed the hungry, visit the imprisoned, comfort those who mourn, help young mothers raise their children, help a neighbor through a sickness, and do so much more in the name of Christ. In this day and age, Christians who are committed to the church need to bear witness to the churchless world around us that Jesus is real and is found within our walls. We need to bear witness to the truth that Christian community is about more than just stewarding traditions or taking care of grandma. The church is a living community through which we encounter our living, resurrected Lord and care for our neighbors in the name of Christ. We need to go a step further than proclaiming, "God is not dead". We need to proclaim that God is alive and is found in the church down the street.

Many are questioning these days, do we really need the church? Much of what we do is formulaic and institutionalized in one way or another. My church, for instance, relies on liturgies and ordos that are inspired by centuries of traditions. It can be a challenge for many my age to see these as anything more than stewarding the past. Other churches claim to be free from religion and only committed to Christ. Yet, like my congregation, they gather at the same time every week, in the same place, using more or less the same instruments in worship, reading the same Bible every week, and have more or less the same expectations about what services will include. In a fast paced world which has changed dramatically in a very short amount of time, it is a fitting question to ponder: can the church keep up? And, does the church have any relevance in our changed world?

If you still go to church, I hope you already have answers to these questions. At the very least, you can attest to the fact that the church is meaningful for you. It is where you find God and where you support your neighbor as you are led by the love of Christ to do. If you are still in the church, you are already a witness to the relevance of the church in a changed world. Though the world around you has changed, the church is still relevant in your life. I encourage you to think about how you might witness to the relevance of the church to people in the world around you. By simply participating in the life of the church regularly and often, you are already a witness to meaningfulness of the church in your life. Keep it up! But, if the church is to survive, those of us in the church need to bear witness to the nature of our communities as instruments of God for a world in need. My generation, on the whole, does not understand why one needs to go to church. Many of us struggle to grasp the reality of God at all, and when we do, we are prone to look for God through the latest Christian podcast rather than through a beleaguered sermon from the pulpit. We have been left to ourselves when answering the question, "Why would somebody go to church?", and the answers that many of us have come up with are that going to church was a practice that was good at one time, but it is no longer. Many of us get lured into the easy answer of thinking that the church is something that is outdated and has been innovated beyond.

I hope you recognize that this Millennial answer to the question of why one would go to church is a terrible answer. There was never a time when church attendance was innovated in. People have always struggled with the question, "Why go to church?" and our responses to the question have long been varied and divergent. Though many people grew up in a time when more Americans went to church than do now, there was no miraculous time in our history when everybody went to church. The highest percentage of people attending church in our country in the last century was 49%. We could not even hit the simple majority of 51%! That was the highest. There has never been a time when the majority of Americans reported going to church on a weekly basis. So, my generation's simple answer of saying, "At one time, everyone thought that going to church was good, but we don't think that way anymore", simply does not add up. The question of why one should go to church has long been an open and dynamic question without simple answers.

More importantly, I believe that people who think about church this way do not understand the pervasive, beautiful, profound nature of what the church is and what the church can be. Those who think that the church has been innovated beyond see the church as a message bearer whose message is now distributed in new ways, with better technology. I won't deny that the message of Jesus' life, death and resurrection is a central element of Christianity which needs to be spoken into our lives regularly and often. I also won't deny that you can receive this message, at least in part, from a daily Bible app which pops up on your phone every morning. But the church is far more than a message center. The church is the place in which we come to worship the risen Lord together and encounter Christ's presence in the midst of worshipping community. The church is the place where we come to die to ourselves in the waters of baptism and rise to new life in Jesus Christ. The church is the place in which we gather together around the table, and share our Lord's body and blood in the bread and the wine. The church is the place where we come together to bring food for the hungry in our towns and cities, gather support for victims of abuse, do what we can to help victims of disaster, and provide a shoulder to cry on for the woman going through a painful divorce. The church is the place in which we form friendships in the light of Christ, become vulnerable before the Lord with one another, and receive forgiveness for the innumerable ways in which we mess our lives up. The church is the place we come to marry the one we love, surrounded by those we love. The church is the place in which we bring our grief over losing family members and others we care about, and be reminded that death has been defeated by the power and love of Christ himself. The church is the place where we bring our children to learn how to hear the Gospel proclaimed over their lives so that they know that their worth does not come from the grades they earn in school or the approval of their peers, but from the love of our God who has formed them in the image of our Creator. The church is the place where we come to learn how to pray, lifting up to God's care those who cannot care for themselves. The church is all of these things and so much more.

As the world changed, many in it have forgotten what the church really was and what the church really can be. As we have looked to the future with eager eyes in order to see what we can do for ourselves, many of us have forgotten how to care for one another in the name of Christ. The church is where this has long happened in profound and pervasive ways, and should always be a place where we care for one another in the name of Christ. So, I believe that those of us who are still in the church are called upon to rise up and bear witness to what the church really is and how God moves in the world through it. We need to articulate who we are, what we do, and how God is present to us in our congregations. Instead of assuming that the world has knowingly walked away from us, we should assume that world has become ignorant of how God is present among us through the church.

Many in the world have been ignoring us for a long time now, so long that they have no idea who the church is anymore. If we do not change how we bear witness to our faith communities out in the world around us, many of our Christian communities will not survive. These are desperate times. When it comes to the church, desperate times call for desperate evangelism. We must actively bear witness to the Christ who saves us, and tell people where to find him – each and every Sunday.

Acknowledgements

I would like to thank the members of Faith Lutheran Church for your support of my ministry endeavors and letting me work out new, crazy ideas with you. Thanks to Dr. Nate Frambach for your timely feedback and encouragement in writing this book. Thanks to my wife Jen for your invaluable love and support as I stumbled along in my efforts to write this book. Finally, I must acknowledge our Creator who has formed us and redeemed us. You renew us through your church and center us as your people.

Bibliography

Kinnaman, David, and Gabe Lyons. *unChristian: What a New Generation Really Thinks About Christianity...and Why It Matters*. Reprint edition. Grand Rapids, Mich.: Baker Books, 2012.

Smith, Christian. *Soul Searching: The Religious and Spiritual Lives of American Teenagers*. Oxford University Press, 2005.

Street, 1615 L., NW, Suite 800 Washington, and DC 20036 202 419 4300 | Main 202 419 4349 | Fax 202 419 4372 | Media Inquiries. "U.S. Public Becoming Less Religious." *Pew Research Center's Religion & Public Life Project*, November 3, 2015. http://www.pewforum.org/2015/11/03/u-s-public-becoming-less-religious/.

Stark, Rodney. *The Triumph of Christianity: How the Jesus Movement Became the World's Largest Religion*. Harper Collins, 2011.

http://www.roman-empire.net/religion/religion.html Accessed January 19, 2016.

Website: http://hirr.hartsem.edu/research/fastfacts/fast_facts.html, Accessed May 5, 2015.

Website: https://www.barna.org/barna-update/millennials/635-5-reasons-millennials-stay-connected-to-church.html, accessed May 5, 2015.

Steinberg, Scott. "Millennial Vs. Boomers: Habits and Characteristics." *Parade*, August 21, 2015. http://parade.com/417128/scott_steinberg/millennial-vs-boomers-habits-and-characteristics/.

"Narcissistic, Broke, and 7 Other Ways to Describe the Millennial Generation [Updated]," April 18, 2013. http://theweek.com/articles/475383/narcissistic-broke-7-other-ways-describe-millennial-generation-updated.

Edwards-Levy, Ariel. "Millennials Are Pretty Terrible, According To A Poll Of Millennials." *The Huffington Post*. Accessed February 3, 2016. http://www.huffingtonpost.com/entry/millennials-poll_us_55e87b8be4b0c818f61b1558.

Stein, Joel. "Millennials: The Me Me Me Generation." *Time*, May 20, 2013. http://time.com/247/millennials-the-me-me-me-generation/.

"Are Millennials as Bad as We Think?" *The Guardian*, January 24, 2014, sec. Media Network. http://www.theguardian.com/media-network/media-network-blog/2014/jan/24/millennials-generation-gap.

Matusow, Allen J. *The Unraveling of America: A History of Liberalism in the 1960s*. Athens, Ga: University of Georgia Press, 2009.

Miller, Claire Cain. "The Divorce Surge Is Over, but the Myth Lives On." *The New York Times*, December 2, 2014. http://www.nytimes.com/2014/12/02/upshot/the-divorce-surge-is-over-but-the-myth-lives-on.html.

Drury, Bob, and Tom Clavin. *The Heart of Everything That Is: The Untold Story of Red Cloud, An American Legend.* Reprint edition. New York: Simon & Schuster, 2014. Page 55, Kindle edition.

http://www.pewforum.org/2015/05/12/americas-changing-religious-landscape/ (Accessed December 2, 2015).

http://www.pewresearch.org/fact-tank/2013/09/13/what-surveys-say-about-worship-attendance-and-why-some-stay-home/ (Accessed 12/2/2015).

http://www.pewforum.org/2015/05/12/americas-changing-religious-landscape/ (Accessed 12/2/2015).

Bolz-Weber, Nadia. *Pastrix: The Cranky, Beautiful Faith of a Sinner & Saint.* 1 edition. Jericho Books, 2013.

Stark, Rodney. *The Triumph of Christianity: How the Jesus Movement Became the World's Largest Religion.* Harper Collins, 2011.

"State by State Data | The Institute For College Access and Success." Accessed May 20, 2016. http://ticas.org/posd/map-state-data-2015.

Martinson, Leslie H. *Batman: The Movie.* Adventure, Comedy, Family, 1966.

Abuse, National Institute on Drug. "Nationwide Trends." Accessed May 5, 2016.

https://www.drugabuse.gov/publications/drugfacts/na
tionwide-trends.

Abuse, National Institute on Drug. "Nationwide Trends."
Accessed May 5, 2016.
https://www.drugabuse.gov/publications/drugfacts/na
tionwide-trends.

"How Will The Shocking Decline Of Christianity In
America Affect The Future Of This Nation?" Accessed
May 11, 2016.
http://endoftheamericandream.com/archives/how-will-
the-shocking-decline-of-christianity-in-america-affect-
the-future-of-this-nation.

Moss, Candida. "Does Christianity Have a Future?" *The
Daily Beast*, April 12, 2015.
http://www.thedailybeast.com/articles/2015/04/12/d
oes-christianity-have-a-future.html.

CNN, Ed Stetzer special to. "No, American Christianity
Is Not Dead." *CNN*. Accessed May 11, 2016.
http://www.cnn.com/2015/05/16/living/christianity-
american-dead/index.html.

"Are We Finally Witnessing The Death Of Christianity In
America?" *Zack Hunt*, December 7, 2015.
http://zackhunt.net/2015/12/07/are-we-finally-
witnessing-the-death-of-christianity-in-america/.

https://www.washingtonpost.com/news/wonk/wp/201
5/06/23/144-years-of-marriage-and-divorce-in-the-
united-states-in-one-chart/ (Accessed April 6, 2016).

Robinson, Anthony B., "What's your passion?", *The
Christian Century*, April 27, 2016, p.11.

"Why Only One in Nine Men Go to Church", Literary Digest, August 31, 1929.

Inc, Gallup. "In U.S., Four in 10 Report Attending Church in Last Week." *Gallup.com.* Accessed May 11, 2016. http://www.gallup.com/poll/166613/four-report-attending-church-last-week.aspx.

Stark, Rodney. *The Triumph of Christianity: How the Jesus Movement Became the World's Largest Religion.* Harper Collins, 2011, pages 185-187.

Constantine the Emperor. Reprint edition. Oxford: Oxford University Press, 2015, pages 148-149.

http://www.roman-empire.net/religion/religion.html Accessed January 19, 2016.

Wilson, Derek. *Charlemagne.* Vintage, 2007.

About the Author

Rev. Seth Nelson grew up in Decorah, Iowa, and now lives in western Montana. He did his undergraduate studies at Valparaiso University and received his Master of Divinity from Wartburg Seminary. He is the pastor of Faith Lutheran Church in Ronan, Montana, at the heart of the Flathead Indian Reservation, where he lives with his wife, Jennifer, their son, Otto, and their dog, Pericles.

Made in the USA
San Bernardino, CA
08 December 2016